PEAK PERFORMANCE IN TENNIS

THE ULTIMATE GUIDE TO
MENTAL FITNESS

Dr. Robert Pasahow

Published by Perform At Peak Press

ISBN: 978-1-941142-75-2

This book is dedicated to my parents Jerry & Lola,
children Joshua, Chelsea and especially my wife Lori,
for making this book possible.

Special Feature

You will see a QR code below. You can take advantage of it. The QR code will enable you to go to a page on my website where videos will make it easier for you to learn how to do the methods taught in this book. You can use any iPad, tablet or phone to watch these videos. If you do not already have a QR code app, you can download an app to enable your device to go to this video page. You can come back to this page anytime you see in the book the following:

Book.PerformAtPeak.com

It is not at all necessary that you use a QR Code. The methods are described in detail and with pictures and illustrations.

TABLE OF CONTENTS

ACKNOWLEDGMENTS

I want to thank all the tennis players, athletes and coaches who have given me the privilege to work with them and help develop Peak Performance Optimization. My clients in psychotherapy and consulting have been an incredible source of information and professional fulfillment. My intelligent and efficient administrative workers have shielded me from distractions that would have drained my energy and time. A special thank you goes to Dr. Debby Vajda and Dr. Fred Gallo for their contributions to help me better articulate the nuances in this field of psychology. Rachel Shuster provided excellent insight, editorial work and research. All the coaches at Quantum Leap, especially Steve Harrison, helped pull me out of the dark ages in my stubborn resistance to social media. Thank you to Chris O'Byrne and JETLAUNCH for their patience, kindness, and professionalism throughout every step of the process. Anis Riana provided an excellent book cover. Denise Cassino's continual access and knowledge provided much information and guidance about social media. This book could have not been completed without the patience and understanding of my family.

CHAPTER 1

MIND OVER MATTER:
GREAT IMPROVEMENT AT BREAKNECK SPEED

We all have had great moments playing tennis in our life. It may have been the time when you played so well that you surprised or even shocked yourself. You could hope or even prayed that you could play like that forever. If there was a bottle that you could store it in, how much would you pay? Were there times when you were close to winning tournaments, but it alluded you? Maybe the great moment came when you won a tournament that you craved to win. Maybe there was a player that you always lost to, and wanted to beat so badly. Players usually think of certain times that they could have played better and won that match. Finally beating that person was a moment of joy and accomplishment. Maybe you did not think that you would continue to play this sport because you were not too good at it. However, there may have been a time period when you finally knew that you started playing well enough that tennis was going to be your lifetime sport. This could have occurred when playing singles or in doubles. Then there is the time when you really knew that you loved this game and hoped that you would play this game forever.

If any of this applies to you, then this is the book for you.

This is the book for players who want to:

- Improve their level of play.
- Play better under pressure.
- Win against players you have been dreaming of beating.
- Not stay upset after hitting a few bad shots.
- Recover better from injuries.
- Learn quicker from your lessons.

This book is for coaches who want to:

- Help your students improve more quickly and easily.
- Be more creative in tailoring your coaching methods on an individual basis.
- Be more effective with athletes who have psychological problems.
- Better deal with difficult parents.
- Decrease their stress and enjoy their job more.

This book is for juniors who want to:

- Improve as quickly as possible.
- Play better under pressure.
- Concentrate better and have less distracting thoughts.
- Improve in the mental aspects of tennis.
- Find a balance among tennis, social activities and school.
- Cope better with the expectations from parents and coaches.

This book is for parents who want to:

- Scale back frustration with their child's rate of improvement.
- Reduce the pressure they're putting on their child.
- Worry less about child's psychological, academic and social life.
- Be less distressed about all that they do for their family or at work.
- Improve their own tennis game.

"The game looks like it takes place between the lines, but it really takes place between your ears."

Novak Djokovic

This book describes a model to better understand psychological functioning and the development of mental skills for tennis players or any athlete. For centuries, dualism was the philosophy and basis for trying to understand human nature. This refers to perceiving individuals as separate entities of the body and mind and not as one. This led psychology to develop theoretical models and experimentation that only examined the nuances of factors affecting and describing the mind as separate from the body. This has been true of western countries compared to eastern. The eastern religion and philosophy of Zen Buddhism has emphasized that the highest states of consciousness can only occur with the transcendence of body and mind.

In the past few decades, western countries' psychologies and philosophies have finally understood the importance of interconnectedness of all aspects of human being and have examined and developed a more comprehensive understanding of human nature and methods to better facilitate the integration of the body and mind.

It is extremely important to understand that any psychological problem incorporates negative aspects of:

> Emotions,
> Thoughts,
> Bodily sensations, and,
> Behavior

All these factors are interrelated and any treatment, intervention, or coaching needs to attend to and resolve all of these components to fully reduce suffering and to optimize functioning. If there is a reduction of a problem, but some negative aspect in thoughts, emotional reactions, psychophysiological sensations or behavior remains then there has not been a full resolution of the problem. Troubling emotions, negative and distorted thinking, psychophysiological disorders, or maladaptive and ineffective behavioral responses do not exist in isolation. Their interrelatedness causes a problem in one component to affect others. There is sometimes an issue of spirituality. Thinking that there is only the body and mind simplifies what indeed exists.

Intense, disturbing and reoccurring arguments with someone provides an example. The thoughts of two people are obviously different and are the basis of the argument. However the differences in thoughts goes beyond that. There can also be thoughts about the other person being stubborn or naïve. Anger and annoyance are usually the main emotions at such times. There can be bodily sensations of tension in the chest or clinching of hands. Problematic behavior could be yelling or interrupting when the other person speaks. Note that the thoughts, emotions bodily sensations, and behavior are happening within a few seconds of each other. If the argument turns out to truly be a very effective communication with mutual agreement and understanding, all of the negative thoughts, emotions, body sensations and behaviors will dissipate. In fact, a transformation occurs. The new emotion could be of appreciation and respect. The behavior can now be improvement at articulating your point without any yelling. Relaxation has replaced tension. When all of this happens at once, the thoughts are no longer experienced as separate from how one feels and behaves. All of you is completely whole, authentic, and integrated, enabling better communication to occur.

For decades, coaching and psychotherapy have overemphasized trying to change a person's thinking and thought problems as the main and first component to elicit improvement for all aspects of psychological problems. When such a method is helpful it typically takes a relatively long time period and some problem remains in one or more of the related emotions, psychophysiological reactions and behavior. For example, the first set of problematic thoughts and reactions are still occurring, but the person has learned how to apply some coping method, such as parroting the words a coach has tried to completely instill. Maybe the person tries to take deep breaths to reduce or tolerate excessively rapid and shallow breathing. However, there still is an internal struggle and tension as such coping methods are applied. In contrast, when all aspects of human experience improve at once, such holistic integration has occurred and coping methods are needed less and, when used, get greater results. In fact, full and simultaneous elimination of all components enables coping strategies to be more effective.

This book describes and teaches the transformative method of Peak Performance Optimization (PPO). Heightened states of consciousness that are rarely experienced can now be deliberately and methodically achieved. This method converts the bad and mediocre to what is great for someone at any moment of or for extended periods of time. Potentialities that reside in oneself that were never seen or even known to exist finally reveal themselves. This is what the great psychologist Abraham Maslow was referring to when he wrote about self-actualization and peak experiences. He described the characteristics of peak experiences, but did not provide a clear path of how to bring it about. Peak Performance Optimization fills this void. It is a methodical series of procedures that enable latent talents to emerge.

This is when a person plays their best tennis.

Interestingly, many individuals may or may not know that such positive change occur simultaneously. The transformation is typically first experienced as a significant reduction or elimination of negative emotions and thoughts. The change in behavior and performance levels are usually experienced or recognized at a later point in time. When it comes to sports, enhanced performance will occur and usually be appreciated upon future reflection. You can only notice the change when you play or compete after applying PPO. There is an additional aspect to the transformation. PPO is so natural that people sometimes do not attribute their improvement to the PPO session. This is known as the "Apex Problem" and will be described in detail later in the book.

In sports, there are different phases of time when one or the other is emphasized. A child or beginner in any sport must start with learning the physical movements of that particular sport. With a child, it starts with a football catch or maybe learning how to throw a baseball with your mom or dad. In tennis, the first thing you may have learned is not to swing the club as if it were a baseball bat. In first learning how to hit a tennis ball, a child probably will hit it over the fence for what he or she thinks is a home run before ever getting close to serving an ace. A child learns to take a club from the ground and then up and backwards before swinging down to hit the tiny white golf ball. Once you start seriously learning a game, you are instructed on the nuances of particular physical movements you need for that sport. A kid in baseball is taught how to hit the ball and how to catch ground balls and fly outs. In golf, there are the different strokes for teeing off, hitting from the fairway, hitting out of a sand trap and, of course, putting. In tennis, you learn how to hit a forehand, a backhand, a volley and a serve, and then graduate to learning to hit with topspin or slice.

The first mental aspects taught in any sport are the rules. From there, you learn useful strategies in that sport. In tennis this includes how to combine serving and volleying, hitting to your opponent's backhand or jumping on a weak second serve. These fundamentals can be learned at tennis clinics or with private instruction from a teaching pro. Many players find they can pick up some aspects of tennis by watching television or instructional videos.

There are numerous books about how to improve in sports. At amazon.com, you will find more than 1,200 instructional books about playing sports. Of those, roughly 150 are instructional books for tennis. There are more than 300 products sold on amazon.com to help you play better tennis, including booklets, DVD teaching aids, different colored tennis balls and arm bands.

Psychologist Mihaly Csikszent described peak performances as an integration of the conscious and subconscious producing physical reactions fully in sync. Whenever there is discussion about peak performance, the idea of being in a zone or flow is inevitably referred to. Flow is the feeling and process when one is performing at their peak. This is a non-ordinary state of consciousness where abilities are far greater than ever realistically imagined. One is fully immersed in a feeling of energized focus, full involvement and fulfilling enjoyment. Csikszent described that flow is a single-minded immersion and represents perhaps the ultimate experience in harnessing the emotions in the service of performing any endeavor. His thoughts attest to the importance of full integration or unification of emotion, thoughts, spirit, behaviors and performance.

It is important to understand the differences between peak performance experiences in sports compared to peak performance over time. Peak performance experiences in sports usually last only a set amount of time. In one NBA game, Kobe Bryant scored 81 points. Klay Thompson recently scored 37 points in one quarter. He did not miss a shot even though he took most from about 23 feet away, He was not a giant in his era as Wilt Chamberlin was when he scored 100 points in a game. However, both were peak performances. A recent example of this is the level of play of Marin Cilic in the semifinal and final matches to win the 2014 U.S. Open. There was no way that any tennis player could have beat him in those two matches, which included a 3 set sweep of Roger Federer, perhaps the greatest men's player of all time. Gale Sayers once scored 6 touchdowns in an NFL game. In modern day baseball,

Felix Hernandez, Roy Halladay, Mike Witt, Tom Browning and Sandy Koufax pitched 1-0 perfect games.

Then there is peak performance that occurs over a time period. Orel Hershiser pitched 59 consecutive innings without the opponent teams scoring even one run. Babe Ruth hit 60 home runs in 1927. The player who had the third most home runs that same year only hit 18. Joe DiMaggio got a hit in 56 consecutive games. Rocky Marciano found a way to win all 49 of his heavyweight career fights, 41 by knockouts. Serena Williams won three of her six U.S. Open singles titles without dropping a set. Byron Nelson won eleven consecutive PGA tournaments in 1945.

For us mere mortals, our peak performances can occur when playing at a level higher than we did in the past or realistically thought was possible. In tennis, maybe you finally beat a nemesis for the first time because you were playing great—not merely because your opponent played poorly. Unforced errors decrease. Great shots and serves happen more frequently. Concentration is not only better, but you are locked in during the points. Emotions do not interfere, but instead engender greater energy and confidence. You can be experiencing a state of being in a zone. Time may seem like it is slowing down, you see the ball more clearly, and your game becomes more effortless

Any explanations about what it was like to be in the zone are usually vague or brief. One has to stay away from falling into the usual conscious states. This is true for all sports. Teammates will sit on the other side of the bench to avoid talking to their pitcher who is in the midst of throwing a no hitter. Kobe Bryant eventually stayed away from the coach and teammates when they huddled together. Conversation would take the person out of this non-ordinary heightened state of being. Amateur athletes tend to make the mistake of focusing on how well that they are playing. Unfortunately, they will not continue to play in their zone.

There is also peak performance for amateurs and the recreational player that occurs over time. In tennis, this involves playing consistently better than previous levels for a period of time, usually for a number of weeks. During this time period, you may not have reached levels of excellence that you had at some point in your lifetime of playing tennis, especially in your younger days when you were much quicker and more agile. With peak performance over time, it is not that you played great every single time, but superior performance is sustained over a number of matches compared to what has occurred in the past.

Throughout the remainder of the book, peak performance in tennis refers to having experiences where you played unbelievably well in a match and/or elevated the level of your game over a period of time.

There are many very good books about improving the mental skills or psychological functioning of anyone playing sports. The goals are very similar and emphasize that you can immensely improve or play at your peak if you:

- Get control of your emotions.
- Not let the nerves get the best of you.
- Control and redirect your anger.
- Block distracting thoughts.
- Employ better strategies and play smarter.

Then there is an emphasis about positive thinking and of inspirational statements, such as:

- Transform desire into will.
- Grab victory from the jaws of defeat.
- You have to believe in yourself.
- You've got to take the initiative to win.

We all know this is easier said than done.

Although some of the ideas and coaching methods are quite good, it is difficult to be doing it when you are out on the court, no less be able to do so quickly. Almost all books, videos and live coaching sessions try to get you to reach these goals through normal conversation, practice sessions, and visualization. And yet, how many times have you been given very good advice, but were unable to follow it? You can be motivated to do what you have been instructed to do but find it difficult to implement. This is true in tennis as in life. This occurs because such teaching methods are directly aimed at the cerebral cortex. This is the outermost and conscious part of our brain. There is much more to the brain.

In contrast, PPO directly and simultaneously stimulates the conscious and unconscious regions of the brain. Sigmund Freud was the great psychiatrist that discovered an entirely new way to understand human nature. Freud observed that there is an unconscious mind and that it greatly affected emotions, thoughts and behavior. In fact, Freud thought of the unconscious as so powerful that his psychotherapy aimed to make what existed in the unconscious to have to get into the conscious mind. Although many of his theories were incorrect, there is no denying the influence of the unconscious mind, in how we think, behave, and perform.

Figure 1 is a graphic illustration of how Freud wanted his students and disciples to think about the functioning of the different regions of the brain.

Figure 1. Freud's view of the conscious and unconscious mind

As Csikszent described, peak performance requires that the conscious and unconscious minds are in sync. PPO is able to do this because it stimulates the emotional and integrative centers of the brain. This very quickly not only affects how you feel, but much more rapidly changes how you think and your ability to benefit from advice and coaching. You come up with the smartest thoughts and strategies and they feel like they're originating from you as opposed to being told to you. You have discovered what is true for you and this occurs quickly.

There is a basic structure to the teaching of the physical and mental aspects in tennis. You are told how to do something new and then repeatedly practice it until it eventually gets incorporated into your game. In contrast, PPO produces a rapid transformation in all psychological aspects that pertain to your tennis game. This enables you to perform at advanced levels when playing.

Although you may believe that the change in your thinking is only occurring in the particular PPO session in the office or over the Internet, it actually will be manifesting when you are out on the court.

You will only Discover that your Past Rate of Progress has been Slow When You Greatly Improve in a Short Period of Time.

Quantum leaps in the rate of improvement can only come from a method that is very different than existing methods, which tend to slowly enable improvement in mental skills and greater proficiency in tennis performance. As such, the PPO system must use methods that are different than those used by other coaching instructors and psychologists who concentrate heavily on the mental aspects of the game. However, introducing completely new concepts, interventions and methods are usually met by skepticism or, worse, dismissal, even before trying them out for a sufficient amount of time. That is a danger and trap that hopefully you will avoid. Buying this book reflects a belief that your tennis game or instruction will improve by learning these methods. As you go through the book, you may feel that your patience is being stretched or tested. There are so many new ideas and procedures. There will likely be times when you suddenly think, "What is he talking about?" At such times take a deep breath, give your mind a little time to think about it and simply follow the instructions. Although it may take you a while to understand all the concepts, you will discover that it eventually is not that hard to do.

"It is important to keep an open mind and never cease to search for new ways of doing things."

Novak Djokovic

PPO has emerged from the field known as Energy Psychology. There are a number of methods and treatment systems. The Association for Comprehensive Energy Psychology (www. Energypsych.org) provides much detailed information about the different methods in this field. Descriptions, videos and a number of instructional materials are provided at this informative web site. Additional information can be obtained from www.tftrx.com, www. emofree.com and www.eftuniverse.com.

The most widely used and researched methods involve acupressure stimulation. Many people think that this means needles are involved. That is acupuncture. Acupressure entails tapping or applying pressure to very specific and energetically powerful acupressure points. PPO incorporates acupressure stimulation through tapping on these important points while simultaneously talking to the client. Imagery is also involved. PPO, as with other energy psychology methods, simply incorporates acupressure stimulation while simultaneously using conventional coaching methods.

Interestingly, when I work with clients in person or over the Internet, it is not necessary for them to totally believe that I will help them. They just have to follow the instructions. When you think about it, it's quite fascinating. We only try brand new methods that we believe have a good chance of being beneficial. Why else would we try it? The expectation that a procedure will work is known as the "placebo effect". The placebo effect engenders improvement that is not the direct result of the method or medicine that is being evaluated for its efficacy. As such, researchers have placebo groups in experiments. Their positive response is then compared to the treatment group in order to isolate the true and specific effect of the treatment.

However, PPO is so powerful that is not necessary for you to believe that it will work. Many professionals in Energy Psychology report that a certain percentage of their clients are reluctant to try such methods because they think that it is strange and do not believe it will work. The only belief that PPO requires is that you follow the instructions that you are given. For those new to receiving such services, motivation and persistence are quite helpful.

A significant amount of information is provided at the website: **PerformAtPeak.com**

You will be able to see videos of the procedures described in the book at: **Book.PerformAtPeak.com**

Being able to refer to your computer will be very helpful in developing your skills of PPO. Tables and forms are available to make it easier to learn.

Chapter 2 is my story which initially led me to be known as a "Psychologist that is in Need of a Psychologist." Trust me, I know what it's like to struggle mentally and emotionally. I was quite deficient in this area, even though I have been a psychologist for decades. I eventually learned techniques that enabled me to discover PPO and my game improved dramatically. I also enjoyed and appreciated the game of tennis more.

Chapter 3 is about the unique aspects of tennis that differentiates it from all other sports. There are many reasons why this is true. Tennis is not a team sport. You are not playing against a field, but the opponent right in front of you. In golf, a pro can bogey the last four holes and be drinking at the bar at the moment that he wins the tournament. All other opponents did not beat the score that the winner may have posted 30 minutes ago. You might rightfully point out that boxing is a one against one sport. However, there are important differences. A boxer does not know the score throughout the boxing match. In fact the score is made by three judges who usually differ from each other. The biggest difference is that a boxer gets advice for one minute from his manager after every round. In tennis, you sit down all alone. In a tournament, your only companions are your water bottle, energy bar, and your towel.

In Chapter 4, you will identify the biggest problems you have in tennis so that you can apply PPO to eliminate them. You will be given a checklist of many possible problems that you wish to eliminate. It is recommended that you try to identify the weaknesses in your game before looking at the checklist. Most people know their biggest weakness. However, going through the list provided might enlighten you to other parts of your game that need to be improved upon.

In chapter 5, you are introduced to concepts that comprise PPO. As I have reiterated, PPO is an entirely different coaching method. It does incorporate techniques used in conventional teaching and coaching. You will learn about the procedures that are unique to PPO. An explanation is given of what is accomplished with each procedure.

Chapter 6 explains the steps you will follow when applying PPO. A PPO session occurs in a specific sequence. Once you learn PPO, you will realize that there are not many steps that are required. In addition, examples illustrate improvement that my past clients have achieved and of steps that were used.

Chapter 7 is when you apply PPO to yourself. You will be taken step-by-step to apply this method. Forms and tables are provided for you to write in your answers. It will probably not be smooth sailing at first. This is because you're going to be learning how to apply an entirely new method. Remember that it probably took a while to master certain strokes in tennis when you first started. Even though you will get a background about PPO, you need to be patient and persist. After doing it a few times, you will get the hang of it. You eventually will be able apply it in a relatively short period of time because your weaknesses are no longer are so weak.

Chapter 8 explains how to fine-tune PPO. Even if you are benefitting a great deal, you still may find it interesting and that certain procedures may help you to be more consistent. If you have improved somewhat, but less than you hoped, you can definitely benefit from the information provided. One section of this chapter is about hypersensitivities, including what you eat. Some of the content of this chapter is about what Novak Djokovic attributes his great improvement to that enabled him to win a number of major championships.

Chapter 9, describes the accession of and Novak Djokovic's tennis career. Although he rose to be the number 3 ranked men's tennis player, Djokovic did not improve for an extended time period. In his book "Serve to Win: The 14 Day Gluten Free Plan for Physical and Mental Excellence" Novak Djokovic wrote about a number of physical and psychological problems he was suffering from. The difficulties that hypersensitivities can cause were described in chapter 8. Gluten was a severe hypersensitivity for Djokovic. A nutritionist used Applied Kinesiology and demonstrated to Djokovic that gluten was physically and psychologically preventing his game from advancing. Djokovic then started a gluten-free diet that he says transformed him and his tennis. He attribute his avoiding gluten as a very important factor that enabled him to become the world's number 1 tennis player.

Chapter 10 emphasizes the need to take lessons. This is especially true when you are trying to change how you serve and stroke the tennis ball. This is due to a phenomenon known as muscle memory. Did you ever wonder why you can ride a bicycle easily even though you have not done so for years? Muscle memory makes it difficult to change a stroke or serve that you have done repeatedly. It becomes deeply ingrained and it is asking too much of PPO to expect this procedure alone can accomplish this goal without taking lessons. PPO facilitates the learning of and the speed that you can make this change.

The next two chapters provide information on the scientific writings, principles and findings that explain why PPO is so tremendously effective.

Chapter 11 provides information about acupressure. PPO incorporates acupressure into conventional coaching methods. PPO does not involve needles as that is done in acupuncture. Keep in mind that the major healthcare system for more than 4,000 years in China was treatments that stimulated the same acupressure system. These procedures have made a major contribution to maintenance of health of the Chinese population, as well as in other Asian countries. It has only been recently discovered that a structured application of this system can enable peak performance in any sport.

Chapter 12 provides information from the field of neurology. Much of the information comes from research demonstrating the discovery of unconscious forces affecting our normal consciousness. It is estimated that there are 1 million cells (neurons) in the brain and anywhere from 10 to 100 billion wires (axons and dendrites) connecting these neurons. There are exponentially more wires emanating from the unconscious that stimulate and influence the conscious region of the brain. Therefore, the unconscious has a very powerful effect. The greatest positive outcome occurs when a coaching method simultaneously affects both regions of the brain. This is exactly what PPO does for an athlete.

Chapter 13 is devoted to examples of how PPO has helped athletes in other sports. This includes golf, baseball, basketball and gymnastics. By no means is this list exhaustive. The examples provided show that whatever the sport is that the PPO method results in superior athletic performance.

Technology has elevated the level of play in tennis. Rackets were originally made from wood that was shaped and glued. Improved metal alloys led to the transition from wood frames to those of metal. However, the technology needed to be developed so that the racket strings could pass around metal wires looped to the frame. The head of the racket eventually increased to almost double of standard wooden brackets. Composite frames were successfully made when carbon fiber and associated manufacturing techniques were developed. Specific areas of the frame could now vary in strength. Different head sizes and the differential weight and balance of a tennis racket became possible.

There are tennis court surfaces that are grass, asphalt, carpet, and acrylic. This has forced players to adjust their strategies and how they play on each of the different surfaces. This probably is the main reason why it is so difficult for professional tennis players to win all four major tournaments that comprise the Grand Slam. The last man to win all four majors in the same calendar year, a grand slam, was Rod Laver back in 1969. Steffi Graf was the last woman who won grand slam back in 1988.

PlaySight (http://www.playsight.com/home) is new technology that has been used in the Air Force and other high profile companies. It provides extensive statistics for a player and coach to analyze after all their matches, enabling the identification of weaknesses, strengths, percentages of winners and unforced errors for each stroke and serve.

There are additional innovations. Chips are embedded in rackets, so that players and coaches can analyze swings. The amount of distance that a player has run over the course of the match can be quantified. Even the spin rates on balls can be obtained. The one technological advance that players and fans benefited the most from is electronic line-calling. This saved arguments and everyone knew that the information was accurate.

PPO represents a new technology for the mental aspect of tennis. Incorporating acupressure into conventional coaching methods is not like any coaching system used in tennis. It has a unique set of procedures that are to be done in standardized ways, while also allowing for flexibility when needed. It brings about improvement at an amount and pace that previously never existed. It quickly enables players to develop or improve in their mental fitness for this sport. Athletes can learn how to apply PPO to themselves. Although there are a number of steps that are new, there actually are not many of them. It is just a matter of learning them through instruction and practice. PPO can be applied days before or during a match. In fact, most of my clients receive services over the Internet and often are nowhere near a tennis court during a PPO session with me. This gives players and coaches' psychological power like they have never experienced before. Once you have received information and instruction from tennis pros, the next crucial step is how fast and how much you improve in the mental aspect of the game such that you play superior tennis.

You should know that PPO also enables you to be at your best in any activity or field related to achievement. Although this book does not devote chapters on how PPO facilitates improvement in your functioning at work, school, public speaking, business, and professional functioning, you can use PPO to make transformations and actualize your latent potential in other areas of life. PPO is a system that is not limited to any one endeavor. Its applications are enormous and effective.

CHAPTER 2

A PSYCHOLOGIST IN NEED OF A PSYCHOLOGIST

Sports was my first love and remains my mistress. I was blessed with good athletic abilities, and fortunate that my parents sent me to sleep away camp that emphasized athletic skills. At the age of 8, I had a rocket arm and became the third baseman of our 10-year-old all-star team. I dreamed that I would one day play in the major leagues. My good fortune continued when I went to a summer camp for four years that was owned by Kutcher's Hotel, which was a mecca for basketball. The late basketball Hall of Famer Wilt Chamberlain worked there as a bellhop when he was a teenager. At night, he played against professional basketball players. He received instructions from the resort's athletics director, the legendary Red Auerbach. Red was the coach of the Boston Celtic teams that won 9 National Basketball Association (NBA) championships in 10 years, an all-time NBA record.

It was at this camp that I saw Chamberlain—whose 100 points in a 1962 NBA game remains a league record—play against Kareem Abdul-Jabbar for the very first time. Abdul-Jabbar would go on to become the leading scorer in NBA history and win six Most

Valuable Player awards. This monumental event was held in the camp's small gym, with not an empty seat to be found.

Then I noticed an old piano in the corner that was right near the court, so I snuck down with my best friend. We sat on top of the piano and were right there, almost courtside, seeing what giants these players were. Electricity was running through my body. Although I was small, I somehow could picture myself dribbling around these guys and scoring. I could even hear the crowd applauding for me. I was a dreamer.

Later that summer I got to see about 20 of the best players in the world playing at Kutcher's Hotel to raise money for the care of Maurice Stokes. A former NBA rookie of the year, Stokes' career had been cut short in the final game of his third season when he hit his head falling to the floor. After the accident, he went into a coma and came out of it permanently paralyzed. Chamberlain, Bob Cousy, and Dolph Schayes were some of the greats in the game. I would imitate them in practice and in games, and in time I became one of the best players for my age. At the age of 11, I lost my interest in baseball, but started dreaming of playing in the National Basketball League.

The next summer, my counselor was Neal Walk. He led all college basketball players in the country in rebounding that next year and was one of the top scorers. He would later become the second player selected in the 1969 NBA draft. Only Kareem Abdul-Jabber was drafted ahead of him. I played under the tutelage of Neal Walk for eight weeks. Needless to say, I got great training on the fundamentals and nuances of the game. Over the years I played and played basketball. Although I was never close to being a great player, I was good enough to become the co-captain of my New York high school team. It wasn't the NBA career I had envisioned, but it was pretty sweet.

I kept playing basketball recreationally and in leagues. My focus in life was my wife and children and developing as a psychologist and researcher. I played basketball whenever I could between work, family and changing diapers. My skills gradually eroded, especially with losing my quickness. I couldn't blow by players off the dribble and just could no longer cover quick point guards. This was a blow to my ego, but a number of factors softened it for me. Most of my friends and I kept getting injured. We kept local surgeons busy. Collectively, my friends had 2 back surgeries, 3 knee surgeries, and a neck injury that ended his career as a dentist. I fractured my Achilles heel (not tendon) and it went undiagnosed for 4 months because the doctors took too few x-rays. I had a number of injuries that I was almost spending more time in physical therapy than on the court. It was pretty discouraging. I eventually realized and told my friends that you either quit basketball before or after a major injury. I played one on one with a kid who was a senior on the local high school team and won 21-18 after hitting a 3 point shot. Although playing against one player is not how basketball is played, but it was the perfect time to give up playing competitive team basketball.

This initially was difficult to accept and I was down and discouraged for a while. Many friends encouraged me to take up golf. I knew that golf posed the challenge of being able to master many different types of shots, would not be so hard on my body, would get to play with my friends, and that golf courses had a special beauty. However, hitting a ball that was not moving and never getting my heart rate over 90 beats a minute was not where it was at for me. I also did not have four hours to play golf at that point in my life.

So I decided to take up tennis. I started making new friends and loved playing outdoors. However, what really appealed to me was that tennis ultimately gave me a new way to let my competitive juices flow. I was now in a sport that involved one on one competition and that tennis required me to learn how to hit many different types of shots. This sport was the perfect transition after playing basketball so long. I liked that tennis involves coordination, skilled shot making and was a way to stay in shape. Compared to basketball, it would be nice not to twist an ankle when landing on an opponent's foot or being hacked while trying to make a layup. I played well under pressure in basketball and 1 knew that being a psychologist gave me the advantage in the many mental aspects of tennis.

I really got into it. I started taking lessons, read many books, watched instructional videos and went away to tennis camps to "learn from some of the best." I traveled to watch many tournament and went to the U.S. Open every year and was in awe watching Borg, Connors, McEnroe, Sampras and Agassi. I saw when Sampras beat Agassi and neither of their service games were broken the entire match. All four sets were decided in tie breakers. All of them were so incredibly talented, quick, and graceful. Like all great athletes in a sport, they made tennis look so easy.

I eventually became obsessed with the game. I played numerous opponents in singles and doubles. I devoted a lot of time to trying to improve different facets of my tennis game. Sometimes it required getting up at 6 A.M in order to fit it into my busy schedule. I always looked forward to my matches and the few tournaments I was in. Although I did not win any, I expected that at some point that I would improve enough to get one. However that is not what was happening. But to my surprise, I was only average. Although I was athletic, the game did not come easily to me. So, I started taking a lot of lessons. I mean lots of lessons from many coaches.

How valuable are lessons?

Consider the following equation:

Amount Improved ÷ Money Paid = The value you get from your lessons.

The idea is for that equation to be as high as possible. That would mean I was improving at a high rate and not spending much money on lessons. That would be getting the biggest bang for the buck. Well, that is not exactly what happened for me.

I cannot even guess how many lessons I took in total, I would estimate that I took lessons from about 12 instructors and went to about 4 weekend clinics. I took more than 20 lessons from one instructor who had previously played on the professional tour and who had a good enough reputation as a coach that he was hired by a group of players and flown to New York to give lessons.

I listened, took notes, and practiced. There were not many topics that I spoke about more frequently. It was behind my family and work and was in third place. I spent a lot more time following tennis and watched more tennis matches on TV than anything else. My wife got rightfully annoyed when I practiced my serve and swings in the house. And that was even before I broke a few vases. When she was out of the house, the racket magically swung again

Although I was getting good instruction and advice, I just was not improving. My biggest problem was the mental side of the game. I was not consistent enough throughout the match and did not maintain my concentration as I should have. I did not play effectively at the end of a close match, which usually ended up in losses. I would make too many unforced errors, whether it was a game where I was serving or returning serve. It was not that my opponents were hitting great shots, but I was giving matches away by not keeping the ball on the court enough or hitting too meekly. I developed a pattern of tightening up and overthinking at some point in the match, especially at the end. I missed too many clear winners when the opportunity aroused and double faulted a bit too frequently. Not that my first and second serves were great, but doubling faulting a bit too much is not exactly a good way to win. Like most people who start developing a negative pattern, a loss of confidence led me to not overcome these difficulties

I wish I could tell you that all these lessons eventually turned around my game. But I just couldn't get the hang of it. It was discouraging and I was quite upset with myself.

Remember that equation?

Amount Improved ÷ Money Paid = The value you get from your lessons.

Whereas I was initially improving very little my play deteriorated such that the equation became a negative number. In other words, I was spending money and only getting worse. My friends knew I was taking a lot of lessons only to get embarrassed as my play did not improve and I was losing too many matches that I should have won. It sucks when four guys play three doubles matches and the only time the three of them lost was when I was their partner.

It killed me that I was losing to guys who were either fat, slow, or uncoordinated. I was much more athletic and in better shape than almost all of them, but I clearly was not winning enough. After I blew a lead and missed a shot to lose another match, a friend sarcastically said to me, "Keep taking lessons. Before you know it, you will be too good to play me." I laughed but I was fuming inside.

There is more to confess. My inability to improve turned me somewhat into a head case. I had a temper. Although players get angry when making mistakes from time to time, I started banging my racket on the court floor or fence. You'd be surprised what shapes a racket can take when you bang it enough. After a while, I broke a few tennis rackets. I can tell you that it takes slamming it about anywhere from one to five times before everything pops. You would think I would have stopped. Rackets are expensive!

Then one day I did something that I am told very few people have done. After missing an easy shot, I threw my racket behind me, the racket spinning towards the fence, Incredibly, the end of the racket grip got stuck in one of those holes in a chained fence—and it stayed there, perfectly parallel to the ground. You cannot imagine how difficult that is to do. We were all amazed. The spell was only broken when a friend said, "That's the best shot I have ever seen you make." I was humiliated, but, in fact, it was the best shot I ever made. I couldn't do that again if I tried a thousand times even if I was aiming.

On a beautiful spring morning, I once cursed so loud playing tennis near some homes that a policeman drove up, walked to our court and admonished me. He told me to stop as there were obviously kids in these homes. He knew that I was a psychologist and pointed out that it wasn't good for a psychologist to be so out of control.

Duh!!! What he said next would become how other players thought of and referred to me. I became known as

"The psychologist who needs a psychologist."

That phrase plagued me and became a good joke for my friends. I loathed it.

Fortunately, around this time, two psychologists recommended that I get coaching from a psychologist who had a great reputation, I learned that his coaching was based on a very different system for helping people using methods that I had not heard or read about before in my decades of being a psychologist. Furthermore, the coach was located more than 2,000 miles away. We were going to do it over the Internet. Naturally this made me more dubious. However, I very much respected my colleague's intelligence and their opinion and got started.

To my surprise and amazement, the coaching helped very quickly. I learned how to apply it to myself. I rarely got too angry and did not let my emotions get in the way of playing smart. It was nice to not have to buy new racquets. I stayed focused and steady in long rallies. Utilizing patterns to construct points and serving effectively was a nice change. I was staying calm, handling the pressure of close matches, winning important points and finally beating players I had not won against before. It was like all the information that my instructors had given me finally sunk into my head and elevated my game

One fat guy used to brag that he always beat me (which he had). Another one said that I would never beat him. They used to get me riled inside. I was dying to beat them. Well sure enough, I beat both of them. In fact, I eventually slaughtered them in a few matches. I cannot begin to tell you how good that felt. How sweet it is.

I got to enjoy this for a while, but then my body betrayed me. Within a three year period, I went through one very painful shoulder surgery and two back surgeries. I was in terrible pain because the disc that is supposed to be between the fourth and fifth vertebrae was not there. This area of my back was bone against bone. To make matters worse, I had spondylolisthesis, which meant that these two vertebrae were not in proper alignment. This resulted in pressure on the nerve roots. It not only caused a lot of pain, but a limp, a condition known as foot drop. The surgery I had was a posterior lumbar decompression fusion. In other words, a section of my back was cut open, bone was filed down, and two vertical brackets were held together by four screws in the bone of my back.

After the first surgery and months of physical therapy, I was once again back to tennis and gradually playing well. However, a new pain developed that was even worse than the first time. I had to have a second more complicated back surgery. This posterior lumbar decompression fusion required dismantling all that apparatus from the first surgery. This time six holes were drilled in my back so that six new screws could be put in the bone of my back to hold the new and longer rods to fuse the third, fourth and fifth vertebrae together.

When I had my follow up appointment with the surgeon, I was warned that I did not have much bone in the three vertebrae. He told me that if I went back to tennis there was a very good chance that the spinal fusions would fail again and could not guarantee me that a third surgery would be successful even if I gave up sports after a third surgery. I was even told that I could not play golf. I could not twist when making a golf swing. The rehabs took forever and were very painful.

Enough is enough. I was done. No more sports. I was deeply upset that a big part of my life was gone forever. I could never run or jump for the rest of my life. I became miserable, high strung, and despondent. Co-workers and my family can tell you that I was unpleasant and upset to be around. I avoided being near tennis courts and did not watch it on television.

I eventually figured out that I should call the sports psychologist again. Although the past sessions had helped me play better tennis, I now had a bigger and more significant problem. I did not know if he could help me. Once again I was surprised. A very important transformation occurred. The four sessions helped improve the way I thought, felt, and made decisions.

This adjustment rekindled my desire to get back into athletics. I simply was going to do it in an entirely new way. I developed and started using Peak Performance Optimization (PPO) based on the same principles and methods that had helped me. I started to be a coach to athletes and consultant to other coaches who were directly working with athletes. PPO improved the psychological aspects of their sport. That resulted in better performance for golfers, baseball and basketball players, gymnasts, and especially tennis players. It helped coaches and teaching pros to be more effective. All of this was occurring in a short period of time, usually taking about one to four sessions. My services gradually expanded to enable businessmen, executives, students, and entrepreneurs to function at a higher level, closer and closer to their peak.

I then realized it was time to pass this information on in a book.

CHAPTER 3

IS TENNIS REALLY THE MOST UNIQUE SPORT?

There are numerous features that are unique to tennis. It is an individual and not a team sport. You can be on a losing team and not have to take the sole blame for your team's loss. Perhaps the place kicker missed two field goals in the middle of a football game or a receiver dropped what would have been an important touchdown. The loss could have many factors such as the quarterback's ineffectiveness or too many turnovers. A baseball team's starting pitcher could have pitched great, but the rest of the team made too many errors. The cleanup hitter may have been hitless in five at-bats, leaving many runners in scoring position. However, the relief pitcher threw one wild pitch and let the other team score too many runs, resulting in the loss. In a post-game press interview, managers and coaches usually point out different reasons why they lost. It is not unusual for the manager to take responsibility for the loss and that makes it less painful for any player to blame themselves.

A point guard in basketball can be blamed for committing too many turnovers. Then there is the infamous missing too many free throws at the end of a game. In fact, the opposing team may purposely foul one of your teammates. Shaquille O'Neal and Dwight Howard certainly have looked responsible for losses when they missed too many free throws. A coach will make it clear that other factors also caused the loss such as poor offensive execution or rotation on defense, and the big man not getting too many rebounds. A hockey goalie can be accountable for allowing too many pucks into the net. However the centers may have lost too many face-offs, or the team never scored a goal, even though they had many opportunities when the other team was shorthanded because of penalties.

Direct competition of one player against another is very infrequent in sports. Golf and many Olympic events are viewed as individual competitions, but any one player does not have just one other competitor. You can have the lowest score in your foursome in golf, but lose the tournament to an individual who you have not seen the entire day. The winner of a professional golf tournament is often not on the course when the moment of victory occurs. This is also true in such Winter Olympic sports as skiing, speed skating, snowboarding, ski jumping, figure skating, luge, and bobsled. Gymnastics, diving, equestrian, and water polo in the Summer Olympics are also decided by the athlete's scores vs. all competitors. One individual may win the tournament, medal, trophy, or prize money, but the athlete is not directly competing against just one opponent.

You could point out that boxing is direct Mano versus Mano, but there are major differences from tennis. A pugilist never knows what the score was for any particular round. In fact, he goes into the last round and does not know the points on the scorecards. He does not know how aggressive to be or that a knockout is required to win. The scores are only revealed when the fight is over, whether by knockout or decision. After the last round, three judges determine the winner. Controversies often erupt when the judges' scores differ substantially from how the announcers and the public viewed the fight.

In tennis, the score is up on the board for all to see during the match. You know exactly what you have to do.

> "It's one-on-one out there, man. There ain't no hiding."
>
> Pete Sampras

There is another very important difference between tennis and boxing. A boxer goes back to his corner and gets advice from the trainer. He can be told why he is being hit so hard and what he has to do differently to knockout his opponent. His cut man treats any lacerations.

All major sports allow athletes to get help from the coach or manager. In a similar fashion, a golfer consults with his or her caddie about which club to use, the wind direction, the conditions of the green, and the break in the green before attempting each shot, to help the golfer make major decisions. This occurs before and during the 18 holes, and possibly for 72 or more strokes in any one round.

Every team sport has a head coach or manager, assistants and trainers who guide the players. Veterans on a team often give advice to a younger player. A pitcher struggling on the mound will often, not only have infielders talk to him, but there is always the reliable pitching coach. The ballplayers have their manager and even a hitting coach. A quarterback not only has a head coach, but the offensive coordinator and even a quarterback coach. Overhead pictures of the defense's formation get to the quarterback to study when he is resting on the bench. Payton Manning frequently benefited from such information. Advice is readily available to a 12 man professional basketball team. It could come from his head coach or one of the four assistants. That is the best ratio of coaches to players in professional sports. Many National Hockey Teams have one head and three assistant coaches on the bench with them. All these games have long pauses for a player to get directions or instruction.

Tennis also is the loneliest of sports. Once the tennis match in a tournament begins, the player is on his or her own. During changeovers, the player sits alone on the sideline and does not have the luxury of getting advice. It's just the player, a towel, and a cool drink.

Even love is bad in tennis.

There are other aspects to tennis that are entirely unique. A tennis professional can have less points in each of the sets and still win a major championship worth millions of dollars. You can win more total points in the match and still lose if you do not get the final point. A player can have a letdown in one set – even lose it 6-0 – and rebound in time to pull out the match.

To earn any set, a player must win at least six games and win by a margin of two games, whether it be 6-4 or 7-5, for example. Sometimes a set is so close that it is only won in a tiebreaker, earning at least seven points and winning by a margin of two, whether it be 7-5 or 8-6. For example, of the last eight men's U.S. Open finals, every match had at least one set go to a tie-breaker. Even though Serena Williams has been so successful in women's tennis, five of the last eight years she won at least one set by the barest of margins. In the last eight years, six finals had at least one of these close sets in the women's French Open. Even through Rafa Nadal is so dominant in the French Open, six of those finals in the last eight years had at minimum one close set. This also occurred in seven of eight years in the men's Australian Open final. In five of the years dating to 2008, four Wimbledon men's champions won by the closest of scores. Amazingly enough, one of these scores occurred in the final set. It took 30 points for Roger Federer to beat Andy Roddick in a tie-breaker in the fifth and deciding set of the 2009 final, 16-14. Such losses can be very deflating and discouraging. Many analysts are of the opinion that this loss was the turning point that led to Roddick's decline and retirement from the game after the 2012 U.S. Open. In those three years before he retired, Roddick mostly remained one of the top players in the world. He still was in great shape, had one of the best serves in the game, won the vast majority of his matches, and was the best American player during these years. No one knows how devastating losing the incredibly close match 2009 caused his early retirement.

Ultimately, the most unique characteristic about tennis: It's the only sport that requires winning the last point.

A football team can win the game even though the opponent has scored the last 17 points. A baseball team can be victorious even if the other team scores the last three runs. Hockey and basketball teams can still win by playing well in the early part of the match even though the other team was quite superior to them for the last half. Not only is it not required to win the last few points as long as your lead holds up, but teams can be crowned world champions even if they played terribly late in the game.

A golfer might be up by a number of strokes and can still win despite playing the last few holes poorly – even recording a bogey on the 18th to an opponent's birdie. Many golfers win and are not even on the golf course, having finished their round and subsequently watching a competitor fail to tie or surpass them. At the moment that you win, you could be drinking a beer and smoking a cigar.

A small percentage of games in sports end up in overtime. It could be argued that it is necessary to get the last point of such games. Yet even in overtime, teams don't necessarily have to win the last point. A baseball team might get three runs in the top of the ninth tenth inning and allow two runs at the end and still win. It doesn't matter even if the two runs came from towering home runs into the upper deck. A basketball team can win in overtime and not score the last seven points. Even in the NFL, a team can win in overtime by scoring on a field goal, as long as it doesn't let the other team subsequently score a touchdown.

Even though boxers are in direct competition in boxing, the circumstances at the end of a boxing match differ from tennis. A boxer, not knowing how the scoring is going, can lose the last three rounds and yet still be victorious. Such boxing greats as Sugar Ray Robinson had six draws and Jake LaMotta had four. Archie Moore had as many as 11.

In tennis, there are no ties; you know exactly what the score is and must win the last point to end the match. It is why TV announcers talk about the ability to close it out for a player going for his or her first major title. As you close out the match, try not to think ahead to what that title can mean for your career. Get the job done first. And it's all on you.

There is no escaping it. Tennis is a uniquely pressure-packed sport.

CHAPTER 4

WHAT IS YOUR ACHILLES HEEL?

Now that I have confessed all the problems that I had in tennis in chapter 2, you get a chance to figure out what your psychological weaknesses are. This is important in order to get the greatest benefit from reading this book. Peak Performance Optimization (PPO) helps to minimize and, even eliminate, your weaknesses in tennis.

When you minimize the worst parts of your game, you move closer to playing at your potential. We usually identify our potential when we remember the best matches we ever played. This almost invariably is a time when you beat someone who you never or rarely had beat before. However, you played so great that time that you won that match. Perhaps you won in straight sets or the only set that you played that time. That would mean you were playing at your peak for most of that match or, at least, for long stretches of it. Maybe you were tied at one set each, but played so great during the deciding set that you can get a glimpse of what it is like to play at your best. For others, it could have been a time when they were behind, but shifted gears, and played so great for the rest of that match that victory was snatched from the jaws of defeat. It may have been when you were playing singles or doubles. If only we could put our greatest tennis playing in a bottle and it be there more often so that we could experience the joy of playing at that level.

The one thing we all know is that we do not consistently play at our optimal level. This is even true with the touring pros in the USTA or ATP. The best players are capable of finding their flow or zone more often. For the club player, there is a larger discrepancy between their usual levels of play compared to when they were playing at their best.

Reducing your psychological weaknesses will enable you to play closer to your potential more consistently. In fact, you may discover that your potential is greater than you ever imagined. You are reading this book to learn how to apply PPO to reach your goals. The most precise and in-depth way to improve your tennis is to start by identifying your weaknesses.

These are a few examples of players who had distinct weaknesses.

A Nervous and Distracted Junior

Christopher was a 17 year old regionally ranked Level I tennis player. Chris was largely taught the game by his father whom Chris idolized. During changeovers, he would think about what his father had taught him. Looking up into the stands and seeing his father had a calming effect. However, Chris was not progressing as fast as his father expected. Chris could tell that his father was frustrated and displeased. A pattern developed where his father would move his hands that Chris easily knew that his father was frustrated with how he was playing. This would upset Chris and it usually led to a deterioration in his level of play. Attempts were made not to look up stands, but were difficult to resist. Then became difficult for Chris to think clearly and come up with strategies when he knew his father was upset with him. It was particularly unpleasant for the days following the tournament when his father, made critical remarks and showed his disappointment.

A Lawyer who Could Not Handle the Pressure

Kurt was a 36 year old lawyer who was quite competitive. He not only was a lawyer, but the top litigator in the firm. He quickly became a partner. Kurt would attribute his success to his ability to handle extreme pressure. In fact, he was one of the youngest lawyers to earn the distinction of being named a Super Lawyer in his city's main magazine. He had a Porsche 911, Rolex Daytona, and "hot wife." He was used to greatness in just about every aspect of his life.

Being quite successful as a lawyer, Kurt expected that he would become very good or even great at tennis. He took many lessons from different instructors, frequently practiced, constantly read books about the sport and trained in the gym to remain fit. All the ingredients were in place. However, he was unhappy about his tennis game. Losing to players he should have beat was quite frustrating. Many times he would not really enjoy playing.

Kurt had two major problems. He had a temper. When, he double faulted or hit unforced errors on easy shots, Kurt would become very frustrated. Instead of focusing on the next points, an internal and critical dialogue would start in his head about how poorly he was playing. Kurt would sometimes start talking out loud and occasionally yell at himself. Keeping with the strategy that he initially intended and maintaining concentration on the next points became impossible. Most of the time his game would go downhill.

His second problem was that he became uptight under the pressure and did not play well at critical points, especially at the end of a match. Winning tiebreakers was especially difficult. He would tense up and start making too many unforced errors. The pressure would get to him. This was an extreme contrast to how he was as a lawyer.

Whereas tennis was supposed to be relaxing and enjoyable, it was disappointing and embarrassing.

An Athlete who was Clutch in Sports

Aaron was a superb athlete growing up. This was true ever since he was young. He usually was one of the best in any sport he played. This included football, basketball, baseball, and soccer.

Aaron would play after school and continually on weekends. One parent would not only make sure he got to wherever his game was played, but made it a point to have at least one if not both would watch his games.

His parents would encourage him and convince other parents and local coaches to allow Aaron to play with older children. This can be difficult for some kids who are used to being the best athlete compared to children their own age. Even at a young age, Aaron enjoyed the challenge of having to play well enough in order to stay up with kids who were older and initially better than him.

Aaron also had a special talent.

He was very good at the end of any sport he was playing. He did better than most in basketball in making a shot towards the end of a game to tie the score or win the game. In baseball he would usually get a hit whenever batting in a close game. Aaron also was the high school field goal kicker in football and dependable at making a field goal towards the end of a game.

Aaron then took up golf at the age of 35 and eventually joined a country club. He once again excelled in this sport and play exceptionally well on the last few holes in a close match. Whereas many golfers become nervous and tense towards the end, Aaron was once again clutch and frequently played well enough on the closing holes to win most matches and even some of the country club's tournaments.

His interest in tennis started in his early forties. Given he was very athletic, worked with a number of teaching pros and frequently played, it was not surprising that he rapidly improved. There were no glaring weaknesses to his game. Except one.

For some unbeknown reason Aaron did not play well at the end of a close tennis match or club tournament. This had never happened before in any sport. For the first time he started losing his confidence and doubting himself.

Methods to Identify your Weaknesses in Tennis

I am making it possible for you to identify your weaknesses two different ways. I highly recommend that you not only do Part 1 first, but that you do it for a while. Almost all players can quickly identify their weaknesses. So Part 1 will not be too difficult.

Space is provided so that you can write your answers in the book. It also would be a good idea to simply photocopy parts one and two. Or bring out the paper and pencil—or your laptop or desktop computer, iPad, iPhone, or anything to jot down your responses to these questions.

You can get this form with the QR.

Part 1:
What are the Major Weaknesses in your Tennis Game?

Write about the worst part of your tennis game that interferes with your level of play and getting better results. Go back and remember the worst experience(s) that you have had on the tennis court related to that weakness. Give yourself some time to think about it. What feelings come up when you think about those experiences and write them down. You can also jot down other bad experiences that you had as a result of this weakness in your tennis game.

_____

_____

_____

_____

_____

_____

Write about the 2nd worst part of your tennis game that interferes with your level of play and getting better results. Go back and remember the worst experience(s) that you have had on the tennis court related to this particular weakness. Give yourself some time to think about it. What feelings come up when you think about those experiences and write them down. You can also jot down other bad experiences that you had as a result of this weakness in your tennis game.

_____

_____

_____

_____

_____

_____

Finish this assignment BEFORE going on to the next part.

Part 2:

Below are lists of problems you might have encountered. Put a check or briefly write about it.

You do not play well enough:

a. _____ At critical points in the match
b. _____ When you are serving
c. _____ When you are returning
d. _____ When your serve is about to be broken
e. _____ The last few games of a tight match
f. _____ At set point
g. _____ At match point
h. _____ Against someone who is much better than you
i. _____ Against someone less talented who you should beat
j. _____ Against the one person you are dying to beat

While playing you display negative patterns:

a. _____ You get off to slow starts and play from behind
b. _____ Starting out well but losing the lead
c. _____ When your game deteriorates after a few bad shots
d. _____ After double-faulting too often
e. _____ After blowing easy shots
f. _____ After blowing a big lead in a game or set

Your thinking while you are playing:

a. _____ Becomes excessively negative
b. _____ Distracts you from concentrating
c. _____ Centers on work problems
d. _____ Centers on worrying about the family
e. _____ Centers on an argument
f. _____ Makes you feel bad
g. _____ Is too self-critical

h. _____ Leads to getting more upset
i. _____ Is about being nervous
j. _____ Is filled with self-doubt
k. _____ Is too much about possibly losing
l. _____ Is about being embarrassed
m. _____ Is about being overwhelmed
n. _____ Is being angry with yourself
o. _____ Is being angry with your opponent

While playing you physically respond by:

a. _____ Being tense too often at important moments
b. _____ Feeling a knot or butterflies in your stomach
c. _____ Feeling fatigued even though you are in shape
d. _____ Giving you headaches
e. _____ Generating jumpiness or jitteriness
f. _____ Gripping the racket too tightly
g. _____ Feeling angry, to the point you could just explode

This book is not just about players. Different groups can experience unique problems and psychological challenges:

Coaches

a. _____ Bored or no longer satisfied with your job
b. _____ Feeling underappreciated
c. _____ Feeling underpaid
d. _____ Fear of losing your job
e. _____ Unsure if you should look for another job
f. _____ Teaching clients you do not like
g. _____ Clients not getting what you are teaching
h. _____ Parents interfering with the juniors you are teaching
i. _____ Parents having unrealistic expectations for their children

Juniors

a. _____ Excessive pressure on yourself to play great
b. _____ Not liking your coach
c. _____ Feeling you're not progressing as fast as others
d. _____ Being pressured and overly criticized by parents
e. _____ Failing to live up to parents' expectations
f. _____ Worrying you are a disappointment to parents
g. _____ Feeling like you are disappointing your coaches
h. _____ Realizing you will never make the professional tour
i. _____ Worrying about the future

Parents

a. _____ Frustrated your child is not playing well or developing enough
b. _____ Worrying you are putting too much pressure on your child
c. _____ Sensing your child is unhappy or overly anxious
d. _____ Sensing your child is losing interest
e. _____ Worrying your child lacks good social relationships
f. _____ Worrying your child is falling behind academically
g. _____ Fearing the outcome of your child being away from home at a tennis academy
h. _____ Neglecting your other children
i. _____ Being overly critical of your children

Doubles players

a. _____ Serving worse than in singles
b. _____ Serving worse from the ad or deuce side
c. _____ Fearing your opponent's return of your serve
d. _____ Doubting your return of serve
e. _____ Difficulty deciding when to come to net
f. _____ Choking when hitting off a lob

g. _____ Worrying about playing with your spouse/intimate partner

h. _____ Worrying about playing against your spouse/intimate partner

The next step is to put your list in order from greatest to least weakness. The checklist in part 2 might make this easier. Give a 1 for your worse weakness, a 2 for the second worse weakness, etc. For now, just put your 5 worse. This will guide you on the order that you should work on these problems so that you will derive the greatest benefits from PPO.

CHAPTER 5

THE FUNDAMENTALS OF THE ULTIMATE MIND-BODY METHOD

The Frustrated Country Club Player: David T, a 45-year-old man, had been an excellent athlete and played college football. After sustaining numerous injuries over the years, he started playing tennis and joined a tennis club.

He took a number of lessons and improved quickly. However, he hit the wall when he was no long getting better. David had always been competitive and this was unacceptable to him, especially when losing to "less athletic, fat, older, and slower players." Working with different instructors and going to weekend camps did not help. He became increasingly frustrated and angry with himself and even stopped playing for four weeks during the summer.

It took three sessions of Peak Performance Optimization (PPO) over the Internet to help him overcome his problems. We first had to treat these recent losses utilizing the Past Perspective Protocol that you will be reading about later. The feeling of being upset reoccurred when he relived those experiences. He then thought about how he would play in future matches and what problems would occur. This is done by using the Future Perspective Protocol that you also will be reading about later.

David stopped getting so upset with himself. He realized that he had never played a racquet sport and was putting excessive demands on himself which only were making matters worse. He took a few lessons from just one instructor, instead of numerous instructors and once again elevated his game and regained his enjoyment of tennis.

Teenager With an Overbearing and Critical father: Seo-yeon, a 17-year-old, was a regionally ranked tennis player. Although her parents could barely afford to get her frequent and great coaching, they made numerous sacrifices. She and her father periodically drove far so she could play tournaments, including trips of more than 1,200 miles. On the longer trips they usually slept in the car. Her father took significant time away from his business, which was an additional cost, and he was not attentive to his other children, who were having personal and school difficulties. Seo-yeon was home-schooled and had very few friends, just acquaintances.

Seo-yeon was talented, practiced frequently, and eventually became highly ranked for her age group. However, she was unable to maintain her rankings, because the pace of her improvement came slowly, even though she was conscientious about practicing and continued to take lessons from instructors.

Seo-yeon idolized her father. Unfortunately he was angry and very disappointed with her. He even humiliated her in front of other players and parents on a couple of occasions. This was greatly upsetting, her level of play, declined and she even considered quitting. Seo-yeon hated it when her parents constantly reminded her how much her family had sacrificed to make her a great player. At times, she was consumed with such thoughts as, "I am no good and I am a loser."

Helping Seo-yeon was not easy. She suffered from a poor self-concept and was plagued by feelings of inadequacy, frustration, anger, guilt, and shame. After five sessions of PPO, she came to understand that her father was living vicariously through her tennis career. Her family harbored unrealistic expectations and were putting her under too much pressure. Her father's criticisms bothered Seo-yeon less and she, in turn, became less self-critical. Although wishing to be a better player, she eventually was satisfied with her game and once again enjoyed playing. When we stopped our meetings via the Internet, Seo-yeon was feeling more positive about herself, developing friendships and even was dating. She was not going to be a professional tour player as she and her father had dreamed of, but she had improved enough that she eventually earned a partial scholarship to college.

What can we learn from these stories? Two different scenarios exemplified how PPO quickly improved these players' games. Some had stopped improving from lessons and resulted in a decline in the level that they played at. PPO not only stopped the downturn, but our PPO sessions refocused them on a new path to improvement. The age and gender of the players did not matter how much they benefited. Progress came in very few sessions, even though most of the sessions were over the Internet.

Many of You do not Realize that your Past Progress has been Slow Because you have Never Experienced Great Improvement in a Short Period of Time.

It is important to understand that PPO is different than conventional instruction and mental skills training. If it were just a refinement of existing methods, the level and speed of improvement described above would not have occurred in so few sessions. This is not meant as a criticism of current teaching methods. Combining PPO with coaching enables tennis players to reach levels they have not ever been at before.

However, the effects of traditional coaching methods are not more efficacious because they do not sufficiently know how to alter the infinitely complex organization of the brain, especially in the limbic system. Methods that incorporate more direct stimulation of the unconscious and conscious mind, such as PPO, make enormous and expedient improvement possible. Recall that interventions need to simultaneously improve emotional reactions, thought patterns, physiological changes, and behavior to bring about exceptional human functioning.

PPO does not replace conventional instruction. Without first teaching the physical and mental aspects of tennis, PPO would be insufficient. PPO simply makes traditional methods more effective. PPO integrates conventional coaching methods with structured tapping of acupressure points. The essence of these methods is used in traditional coaching and therapy. An explanation of concepts and methods unique to acupressure based methods will subsequently be provided. Many of the concepts and definitions below will be new and may seem incredulous to you, but will help you to understand the procedures of PPO.

I cannot emphasize enough that these methods have to be dissimilar to conventional coaching techniques in order to get exceptional results. The integration of conventional and acupressure based methods enables PPO to quickly engender large amounts of improvement in short periods of time.

> "Without an open mind, you can never be a great success."
> Martha Stewart

The only way that you will discover that your performance on the tennis court increases a few notches, as described in the above stories is to simply follow the instructions when applying PPO. One needs to be open to the possibility that such results are possible. There is no placebo effect. This is another special feature of PPO. You will get the best results by accurately doing methods described.

The videos that you will be able to watch at **Book.PerformAtPeak.com** will make it easier.

Methods of PPO that are Similar to Conventional Coaching

Selection and Activation of the Problem: In the previous chapter, you focused on the problem that you want to reduce. The next step in PPO is to psychologically activate the problem. This is done by thinking about and picturing by using imagery about the problem in your mind. A choice first must be made whether you will think about the problem in the future or past.

The following guidelines help you make this decision.

If the problem is longstanding, you will probably have to initially focus on past negative experiences. This is because those upsetting times curtail your capacity to improve in the mental and physical aspects of your tennis game. Although you may not have thought about those upsetting experiences in a long time, it does not mean that they are not currently restricting your level of play.

Most of my clients want immediate results. As such, they will apply PPO by thinking that their problem will occur in the future. This means that they are trying to change the mental aspects of their game with it subsequently eliciting improvement of how well they perform in their next matches. However, if applying the Future Perspective Protocol does not bring about improvement then you should follow the guidelines of the Past Perspective Protocol.

Whenever activating a problem when thinking about it in the past or future, negative emotions or body sensations are experienced. Such feelings comprise the distress that you are experiencing at the moment. Thus, any negative feelings should be thought of as distress and are to be rated.

Distress Rating: Distress is the word that will be used to reflect the intensity of your negative emotions and body sensations. This is called a Distress Rating.

Ratings are given on a scale of 0-10, where 10 means you are experiencing the most intense emotion or sensation as you ever have in your life. A 5 would mean that you are experiencing half of the distress of that intensity. The 0 rating signifies that the emotion or bodily sensations are not evident; even though you are thinking about that problem. To help you better understand how to give a Distress Rating, think about something or event that you are worried about. It could be about work or one of your children. Maybe you will experience greater distress if you think about an event that was very upsetting from the past. Notice how you feel right now at this moment. How strongly are you feeling it? You would then rate that intensity from 0-10. It is very important that your rating be about the moment that you are doing PPO, *not* about how you think or imagine you might have in the future. Think about the problem and notice what you are feeling at the moment.

Example of Distress About a Future Perspective: Kenny was satisfied with all aspects of his tennis game, except for his backhand. He wanted to improve it. When he thought of having the problem when playing important matches in the future, the nervousness that he felt at the moment of thinking about this problem was a 6.

Example of Distress About a Past Experience: Amy became anxious when playing poorly in mixed doubles, especially when teamed with someone she did have a former connection with. She had a number of past experiences that were upsetting to her. When Amy thought about the worst one, she felt a knot in her stomach and rated the intensity of this body sensation as a 7.

Emotions and Body Sensations: When doing PPO you will experience negative emotions or body sensations after activating the problem. It is best if you can identify the emotions or body sensations at these times.

Here are emotions and their associated negative body sensations that most commonly limit how well you play in tennis or learn from lessons:

Nervousness: This is an uncomfortable and unpleasant state characterized by feelings of agitation, uneasiness, jitteriness and anxiety. Nervousness tends to occur at important moments in a tennis match. Bodily sensations that can occur with nervousness are feelings of butterflies in the stomach, tightening up or heart racing. Some people refer to these experiences as anxiety.

Apprehension: A feeling of dread, foreboding or trepidation. It is similar to nervousness, but tends to be elicited more by worrying about a future tennis match. One might be apprehensive the night before a match and sleep poorly. Bodily sensations that can occur with apprehension are similar to anxiety but tend to be less intense and are usually felt before the match begins.

Anger and Rage: A feeling of being intensely mad, irritated, annoyed or agitated. Body sensations that occur with rage are intense tension throughout the body, clenching hands or squeezing the racquet. It can be manifested in such behaviors as outbursts, cursing, smashing or throwing a racquet.

Being Discouraged: A feeling of being deterred, depressed, pessimistic or beat down. A bodily sensation that can occur with being discouraged is a feeling of heaviness and weakness. Subsequent play is less energetic and concentration decreases. You might think that losing in the current match that you are playing is inevitable. You might find that you are not even trying to play at your best.

Embarrassment: A feeling of humiliation, bashfulness, awkwardness, or timidity. Bodily sensations that can occur with embarrassment are a feeling of being hot or flushed or a strong desire to not look directly at others.

Shame: a feeling that is very similar to embarrassment. The major difference is that you are more upset with yourself than the fact that others see or know that you played poorly.

Important to Keep in Mind: It is not necessary to entirely understand and do the steps that are described below. You will be given very detailed instructions on how to do PPO in the next chapter. It will help that you get familiarized with PPO.

Concepts and Procedures of PPO That are Different from Conventional Coaching

The Chinese Acupressure System: The underlying processes and methods that are used in PPO come from the same system that underlies acupressure and acupuncture. It does not involve needles as in acupuncture. There are a number of ways to stimulate the acupressure system. In PPO, we are just activating it by tapping on specific acupressure points. Tapping is the predominant manner that Energy Psychology Methods utilize.

The tapping of specific acupressure points decreases negative emotions, thoughts and bodily sensations. It requires not only that particular acupressure points are tapped, but the sequence that they are tapped is what is important to resolving any problem and reaching any particular goal. This is the basis of why acupressure-based therapies are so effective in reducing psychological and emotional disorders and symptoms, which further helps a great array of different problems for people of any age.

One of the applications of acupressure-based therapies, such as PPO, is that it affects all of the above factors that can lead to outstanding results. This is true for many endeavors related to performance. For instance, PPO is effective with elevated performance in any sport. This is also true in raising the functioning level in any field, such as business, medicine, law, and almost all other occupations. It helps students to have less anxiety and achieve higher scores in any important Scholastic tests, such as the SAT, ACT, and GRE tests, in addition to various boards that need to be passed in order to get a license. PPO also helps to tap into the creativity of many areas, such as the writing of articles, books, music, and poetry. Learning and applying PPO will enable your innate talents to reach the highest levels of achievement. People reach what they thought their potential was only to discover that they are capable of more.

Emotions are Associated with Specific Acupressure Points: Any negative emotion can be reduced with the proper application of acupressure. A comprehensive list of feelings can be differentiated and put into different groups that have common themes.

Anger, frustration, annoyance, enmity and rage are similar in nature. Sadness, depression despair, grief, despondency, hopelessness, helplessness, remorse sorrow, misery, anguish and apathy can be grouped together. Anxiety, apprehension, nervousness, and panic are related emotions. Embarrassment, shame, guilt, humiliation, and shyness have some similarity.

Emotions that Interfere with Performance in Sports: The above group of emotions that impede athletic achievement can be simplified. The ones that athletes tend to feel and label the most are:

Anxiety
Nervousness
Apprehension
Anger
Frustration
Rage
Discouragement
Sad
Embarrassment
Shame

Not everybody has all of the emotions listed above. That does not matter. In some ways, that will make it easier for you to apply PPO.

Acupressure Points Reduce Negative Emotions: All of the above negative emotions can be decreased by applying PPO. This requires tapping specific sequences of acupressure points.You will receive a narrative detailed description and visual chart of the location of the acupressure points in the next two chapters.

Comprehensive Acupressure Tapping Sequence: (CATS) This refers to the tapping of a sequence of acupressure points to decrease negative emotional states or body sensations. There are a number of clinicians and coaches in the field of Energy Psychology who believe that different emotional states require tapping a different order of acupressure points than CATS. More details about this information will be described in chapter 8. For now, applying CATS will make PPO easier to learn. Another reason that learning CATS is helpful is because some individuals feel bad or upset, but are unable to label the specific emotion that they are experiencing.

Applied Kinesiology: This is a procedure that provides information about the interrelationship of the mind and body. Applied Kinesiology has been utilized to obtain information in many fields, most commonly to assess and treat pain and to test allergies to food and nutrients Applied Kinesiology is utilized in a number of different Energy Psychotherapies. Callahan was the first to use Applied Kinesiology in Energy Psychology and used this method to assess and confirm treatment procedures and their effects. In Applied Kinesiology, the therapist or coach applies a consistent amount of force to a specific muscle of the client (referred to as the indicator muscle) while the client resists movement of this muscle with the same amount of strength at all times. The weakening of the indicator muscle, even though the client is given the same resistance, provides diagnostic information. More experiments need to be conducted to better understand the efficacy of this procedure.

Clinicians and coaches have found this to be a useful assessment method to provide information about the body-mind connection.

Psychological Reversals: Psychological Reversal has been one of the most important discoveries in the field of Energy Psychology. Since this is a very important concept that almost all people are unfamiliar with, there will be a very detailed description of this phenomenon.

Psychological Reversals are an unconscious, powerful and energetic force that is inherent and part of any important and difficult psychological dilemma. It causes you to have negative thoughts and emotions and often leads to self-defeating behavior. You can have a clear goal in mind, but find yourself acting in a way that is directly opposite of your intentions. The word "reversal" in Psychological Reversal is not random, but reflects how the body and mind work in opposite ways. This makes it almost impossible to overcome a problem.

An example is when overweight people try to lose weight and spend a great deal of money in different programs to overcome this problem. Although they are extremely motivated when you speak to them, their eating pattern periodically is the opposite of what their intentions are. They know they are eating the wrong foods and binging and that prevents them from losing weight. They usually have no or a distorted idea why they are doing this and feel helpless to stop this self-defeating behavior. Their overeating makes others perceive them as unauthentic or not in touch with who they really are. However, the Psychological Reversal precludes them from consistently avoiding binging, overeating or eating high-caloric foods. They know what their intention is, but are helpless and perplexed as to why they cannot stop.

Note that this phenomenon has the word "Reversal". This force may not necessarily elicit self-defeating behavior, but it can cause people to progress slowly or not at all when doing any intervention or when taking lessons. Distress Ratings are reduced slowly and not completely and precludes the elimination or significant reduction of the problem. In such cases, Psychological Reversals are to be thought of as an impediment that obstructs people from improving on or reaching their goals. A person can be extremely motivated but find themselves progressing very slowly even if they are expending tremendous effort.

Figure 1: Similarity to a Psychological Reversal

The picture in Figure 1 is analogous to a Psychological Reversal. The reversal is represented by the boulder. It makes going up the steep hill almost impossible. In fact, it could cause him to fall down the hill and cause him to go the opposite direction of what he intended. The man will not get to his destination or goal of being at the top of the hill. Removing the boulder will make it less difficult. He will still have to walk up this hill, but it will now be easier. After eliminating a Psychological Reversal, tapping on a sequence of acupressure points still has to be done to eliminate the problem.

As such it is important to get rid of the Psychological Reversals right at the beginning with the application of treatment steps of PPO. If a Psychological Reversal exists, the tapping of a sequence of acupressure points only becomes completely effective after eliminating the Psychological Reversals.

As is true in life, Psychological Reversals prevent you from reaching your goals in tennis. The following are examples of how Psychological Reversal are likely to be occurring in tennis:

- You are playing well the entire match and then all of a sudden you start playing poorly.
- You find yourself having many irrelevant thoughts about the match and being unable to keep your head in the game.
- You are playing poorly throughout an entire match and have no clue why this is occurring.
- At the end of close matches, you play worse than what you expect and want.
- You feel too nervous or angry at yourself and it causes you to play worse than you really should or expect.

A likely example of the existence of Psychological Reversals in professional tennis occurred, believe it or not, with Novak Djokovic, who at the time of this book's publication was the number 1 player in men's tennis. For a long time Djokovic was known for losing focus or stamina. He turned pro in 2003, at 16, and did not win his first title until 2006. In 2009 he retired in the fourth set of the Australian Open quarterfinals, lost in consecutive sets in the round of 32 at the French Open, lost in four sets in the Wimbledon quarterfinals and lost in straight sets in the U.S. Open semifinals. In 2010, he lost a five-set match in the Australian Open quarterfinals, a five-set match in the French Open quarterfinals and a straight-set match in the Wimbledon semifinals before his four-set loss to Nadal in the U.S. Open finals. He clearly looked like the superior player in some of these matches but just could not win.

He did not win his first grand slam championship until the 2008 Australian Open—then didn't reach even the final of another major championship until losing to Rafael Nadal at the 2010 U.S. Open. It is hypothesized by others and myself that a Psychological Reversal contributed to this wonderfully talented player's problems.

Finally, in 2011, Djokovic won his second, third and fourth major titles, at the Australian Open, Wimbledon and U.S. Open, on his way to seven career grand slam titles. In his book, "Serve to Win" Djokovic clearly explains dietary factors caused his problems. His dietary problems are an example of an obstructive force known as "Energetic Hypersensitivities" These Energetic Hypersensitivities caused a loss in stamina and a decreased level of play. Energetic Hypersensitivities cause Psychological Reversals and are explained in detail in Chapter 8 on Troubleshooting and Refining Peak Performance Optimization.

Coaches have not been trained to detect when this obstructive force exists in a student they are instructing and who is improving very slowly or not at all. This is true with tennis players at all levels. This is indeed unfortunate because a coach who is very skilled can be blocked from being more effective. This sometimes leads players to prematurely stop taking lessons. Psychological Reversals limit the performance of any athlete.

Indications that a Psychological Reversal is present in a coach include:

- Losing your interest in coaching.
- Getting very annoyed and impatient with one or a few of your students, but not all.
- No longer trying to improve or educate yourself as a coach.
- Feeling like you are having a bad day and just want to go home.

You can more easily learn how to do certain procedures in PPO by going to a computer, tablet, or phone and go to review the videos during or after reading about a specific procedure.

The power of Psychological Reversals can be understood more clearly from the video on my website.

You can use the QR code to the right to go to my website to view the video.

Video of Psychological Reversals and Eliminating Psychological Reversals: The woman in this video on the website is holding her arm straight out to the side. I am pushing her arm down with the same amount of force each time. She resists my pushing down of her arm with the same strength each time as well. She is using about one half of her strength to resist my pushing her arm down. Note that she has less physical strength and that her arm goes down when making a positive statement, such as, "I want to be over this problem," compared to saying, "I want to keep this problem." In fact, every muscle in her body would have less strength when verbalizing, "I want to be over this problem." It is not that she wants to keep this problem. We know that this would not make any sense in any discussion. However, she had a Psychological Reversal and this caused her arm to be weaker when saying "I want to be over this problem." In fact, every muscle in her body would show this reversed differential strength.

Do you think she, or you, could quickly benefit from coaching when every muscle in the body is stronger when thinking of wanting to keep this problem compared to wanting to be over this problem? You can be receiving great instruction from a tennis pro that you totally agree with, but are unable to implement it into your actual playing on the court or maintain any improvement.

You can also see in this video an example of a future reversal. The woman's arm is stronger when saying "I will continue to have this problem" compared to "I will be over this problem."

Notice how easily a Psychological Reversal can be removed when tapping the correct acupressure point. This will be explained in detail later in this chapter.

Psychological Reversals exist because there are unconsciously wired connections in the subconscious and conscious regions of the brain that cause and maintain these powerful obstructive forces. The fact that there are more wires or projections going from the subconscious to the conscious mind compared to the opposite explains why such self-defeating behavior occurs and persists. The phrase "Body-Mind Connection" is frequently referred to in psychology, healthcare and alternative medical methods, to partially explain diseases. Psychological Reversals may be the best example of how the body and mind are working in opposite directions.

There a number of different Psychological Reversals. They are known as: Major Reversal, Specific Reversal, and Future Reversal.

A Major Reversal exists when you play poorly all match, are aggravated with yourself, are not concentrating well and not enjoying playing.

A Specific Reversal is limited to an aspect of your game. After taking many lessons, you never improve your backhand, for example.

A Future Reversal exists when you temporally improve, but have a reoccurring problem and you start playing poorly again.

There are also thematic-based reversals that are discussed in chapter 8.

Treatments for the Reversals: The great news is that these powerful Psychological Reversals can be quickly eliminated by tapping on the correct acupressure points. The undoing of the reversals simply occurred by tapping on the correct acupressure points. Sometimes an affirmation about self-acceptance needs to be verbalized three times when tapping the specific areas on the body or face. Sometimes tapping on the acupressure point is sufficient. All Psychological Reversals can usually be eliminated in a few seconds. The next chapter will specify how this is done.

Brain Balance Procedure: This is a nine-step procedure that stimulates the different regions of the brain. This method has integrative properties that further reduce the intensity of negative emotions and body sensations. Note that the 10th acupressure point is tapped on throughout this procedure.

Tapping Rounds: Once activating the problem and giving a Distress Rating, a Tapping Round is applied by:

1) Tapping the acupressure points to eliminate potential Psychological Reversals
   Give a Distress Rating
2) Applying the Comprehensive Acupressure Tapping Sequence (CATS).
   Give a Distress Rating.
3) Doing the Brain Balance Procedure
   Give a Distress Rating.
4) Applying the Comprehensive Acupressure Tapping Sequence (CATS).
   Give a Distress Rating

A Tapping Round is simply these 4 steps. A number of tapping rounds are done in the PPO procedure. Once you do PPO a number of times it will take you under 2 minutes to do one round. In the beginning it will take longer as you learn how to apply this method. With each round, simply note current distress at the moment and give it a Distress Rating. It is recommended that you do at least three rounds of the same exact steps described above.

Aspects: Aspects are smaller parts of a psychological or performance problem. This is usually a previous upsetting experience, negative thoughts or additional emotions that were not identified when initially thinking about the problem. Recall that a psychological problem has the following components: negative emotions, body sensations, thoughts, behaviors and decision-making. These components have to be attended to in order for there to be a resolution or elimination of a problem.

It is not unusual to experience different emotions or body sensations when a new aspect or prior experience occurs. You will simply apply three rounds of PPO, changing the acupressure points associated with the new emotion in steps 2 and 4 of a PPO round.

Example of an Aspect: Alex, a 17 year old, became very apprehensive before his high school matches. Although he had a very good record, he always felt nervous, even days before a match. He started tapping the acupressure points associated with anxiety. During the session, he had memories of his father admonishing him when he lost matches. He felt shame when reliving those experiences and then tapped in steps 2 and 4 of a PPO round a different set of acupressure points, those associated with shame. A session was devoted to eliminating the disturbing feelings he had about these experiences; only then did a session focused on being less anxious subsequently help him to improve.

Peak Performance Optimization (PPO): A number of tapping rounds are done in PPO. This includes all the tapping to eliminate Psychological Reversals, the sequence of acupressure points tapped associated with your negative emotions, and the Brain Balance Procedure. A repetition of rounds occurs in a PPO session until the Distress Ratings are as low as possible. Rounds can be devoted to reducing related aspects of the problem. PPO also includes additional procedures that you may use as you refine your skills in doing PPO.

Complete Zero: This refers to when you are not having any disturbing emotions or negative feelings even though you try to think about, picture or remember the problem when you first started the PPO.

If you are at complete zero, it almost invariably reflects that you have decreased the problem as much as possible during your session. In fact, it may now be eliminated. It is not unusual to feel totally relaxed or fatigued at such moments. You may even yawn. Sometimes you are unable to think about or picture the problem even though you try to recall it. Reaching complete zero is the goal of any session

Self-Advice: There is a time when you give yourself advice overcoming the problem during a PPO session. This occurs when you are tapping on acupressure point 10 for a while. The thoughts you have at this time are very accurate, positive and useful as a guide when you are subsequently playing.

Eye Roll: This brief step is done when the Distress Rating is a 1 or 2. This is a method of lowering your Distress Rating, hopefully to 0. It involves continuously tapping on the acupressure point 10 for about five seconds. At the same time, you close your eyes, open them to look at the floor and then move your eyes to the ceiling without moving your head.

The next two phenomenon do not occur within in a tapping round. These phenomenon occur after you have completed PPO and significantly reduced your Distress Rating.

Generalization Effect: Generalization occurs when a Distress or Rating significantly decreases when applying PPO. The decrease of negative feelings in the session results in an improvement on the court. However, the generalization effect goes beyond that. When you get your Distress Ratings very low PPO not only reduces the problem you focused on, but will probably help other related facets of your game.

Example of the Generalization Effect: Ellen felt nervous when thinking about approaching the net when playing doubles. Her anxiety was 5 at the beginning of the PPO session and was then reduced to 0. When subsequently playing, she not only felt less nervous when playing towards the net, but also resulted in her getting more of her first serves in and improved her volleys. We never focused on the serve or the volley in the session. Nevertheless, the generalized effect from PPO resulted in these additional benefits.

Apex Problem: This is an extremely important phenomenon.

This occurs when a client accurately reports that the desired goal has occurred, but does not attribute his or her improvement to the PPO intervention. An individual may have taken lessons and not improved and subsequently improves after a PPO session. Some clients end up thinking that PPO had very little to do with their progress. They may credit their improvement to having discussed the problem. This even occurs when we had an earlier session talking about the problem and little or no improvement occurred. It was only when the method was applied that the desired goal was achieved. The reduction of distress comes so easily that it now feels like a natural part of you. It is so smooth that it is possible to not attribute the improvement to the session.

The Apex Problem presents an important problem. You may have progressed in how you think and react on the court after a PPO session. Sometime later you may want to elevate some other parts of the mental processes or your performance level and become unsuccessful. It may not occur to you to apply PPO again. This happens when you do not realize that it was PPO that made such a large and quick improvement possible. You can also learn how to apply PPO on yourself. However, if you do not attribute your improvement to the method, there is little or no motivation to learn, memorize, and use it.

This chapter introduced you to a number of new concepts. As stated before, methods to bring about great improvement quickly must be different than traditional coaching methods. It is not necessary that you totally understand or memorize, at this time, all of these concepts and definitions in this chapter.

The only way that you can test whether you will be able to improve, as in the aforementioned stories, is to follow the instructions when applying this method. You simply just have to follow the procedures.

The sequence of steps of how these concepts and procedures are applied is described in the next chapter. It is your passageway for rapid improvement in order to reach your goals.

For the picture of the man pushing the boulder, he is at the top of the hill enjoying the view. It was even more beautiful than what he anticipated.

CHAPTER 6

THE STEPS OF A PEAK PERFORMANCE OPTIMIZATION SESSION

Now that you have been introduced to the concepts of Peak Performance Optimization (PPO), it is time for you to learn the sequence of a PPO session, whether it is being done on you by someone or you are applying it to yourself. This chapter will help you to become more proficient in this method and derive greater benefits.

Even though you may be eager to apply this method, it is highly recommended that you read this chapter first before going on to the next chapter about self-application of PPO. A very detailed step-by-step description will guide you toward decreasing or removing the worst parts of your game. Moreover, you will discover that there are additional ways to apply PPO to further elevate your game.

Selection and Activation of the Problem

The first step in PPO is to pick the weakness in your game that you want to eliminate. You have already pinpointed that in chapter 4.

As previously described, you must choose whether to apply PPO by taking a future perspective or recognizing that you first must eliminate the negative effects of past experiences that would impede your rate of improvement. The Future and Past Perspective Protocols are:

Future Perspective Protocol: Take some time and imagine what it would be like for your problem to be present in a future match that is important to you. To activate the problem, you first need to think about and picture that you are playing great tennis and that your problem is now occurring. It may help to think about when you played the best tennis in your life and project that you will replicate that in an upcoming match that you care about. Now, think about and picture that your problem has started. You are playing poorly, losing points that you shouldn't have, and everything you try is not helping. As you are doing this, notice what negative emotions and bodily sensations you are feeling at this exact moment.

If you are currently not experiencing any negative emotions or body sensations, add another potentially upsetting aspect. For example, picturing yourself serving poorly is not generating any negative feelings. However, if you think about serving poorly, how it's costing you the match *and* that your friends are watching, you will more likely experience negative emotions or body sensations. The feeling you will then have while thinking about and picturing that is referred to as "Distress." The intensity of this distress then gets rated.

Past Perspective Protocol: Sometimes applying PPO using a future perspective does not help enough or at all. There are two ways that you will know that this is occurring: 1) You did not reduce your Distress Rating to 2 or below when using the Future Perspective Protocol when applying PPO; 2) You did eliminate the distress in your PPO session, but it did not help when you subsequently played, especially if you took lessons soon after doing PPO.

The most frequent reason that PPO does not work is that you have had too many upsetting experiences in the past. The first step is to think about your problem and identify the two most upsetting past experiences that you have had in tennis.

When applying the Past Perspective Protocol, you are to try to re-experience the upsetting event as deeply as you can. The idea is to activate the problem as much as possible so that it elicits negative feelings. It helps to think about and picture the experience. You'll know when you have activated the problem when you feel negative emotions or body sensations.

Start with the most upsetting experience you have had in tennis and think about and picture it. Try to re-experience it as if it just happened. The feeling you will then have while thinking about and picturing that is referred to as "Distress." The intensity of this distress then gets rated.

Transition of Past Perspective to Future Perspective Protocol: Once you substantially reduce or eliminate the negative feelings from the past experiences (i.e. Distress Ratings =0-10), you then apply PPO with the Future Perspective Protocol.

Distress Ratings: When doing a PPO session, you will feel distress at different times. Ratings are given on a scale of 0-10, where 10 means you are experiencing the emotion or sensation as intensely as you ever have in your life. A rating of 0 means that you no longer have that emotion or bodily sensation even though you are thinking about that problem. It is very important that your rating be about the moment, not about how you think or imagine you might in the future. Likewise your Distress Rating when thinking about past upsetting experiences is the intensity that you feel when doing PPO. Your rating is not about what you felt when going through that experience at that time. You are to think about the problem and notice what you are feeling at the moment.

A Round of PPO: Once you have activated distress and have given it a rating, you do a round of PPO. This consists of

1) Tapping the acupressure points to eliminate potential Psychological Reversals.
2) Tapping the Comprehensive Acupressure Tapping Sequence (see below).
3) Doing the Brain Balance Procedure.
4) Tapping the Comprehensive Acupressure Tapping Sequence (see below).

All these steps are described below in detail.

A Distress Rating is given before and after the 4 steps.

Eliminating Psychological Reversals

Recall that Psychological Reversals can prevent PPO from working and must be eliminated right at the beginning of the session. Below are the steps that you will follow to eliminate the Psychological Reversals. There is no need to follow the procedures now. This is just to familiarize you with them. The location of the acupressure points is on page 72.

Tap on the karate spot (Acupressure Point 1) and say three times: "I deeply and profoundly accept myself with all my problems and limitations."

This eliminates the Massive Reversal.

Pause a few seconds. Tap on the karate spot (Acupressure Point 1) and say three times: "Even though I have this problem, I deeply accept myself."

This eliminates the Specific Reversal.

Tap under your nose (Acupressure Point 2) and say three times: "I deeply accept myself even if I never get completely over this problem."

This eliminates the Future Reversal.

After completing one round, treating the Specific Reversal is done in subsequent rounds. You do not have to keep treating the Massive and Future Reversals.

You would then write down your Distress Rating. Don't be surprised if it has not gone down. Elimination of the reversals makes it easier for all the other steps to decrease distress. Recall that the man will not be further up the hill when the boulder is removed. However, he will be able to more easily make progress up the hill when that boulder has been removed.

Difficulties saying "I deeply accept myself." The statement of accepting yourself is known as an affirmation. Other coaching and therapy methods have people make these affirmations, maybe you have done this yourself. Just doing affirmations usually makes one feel better in the short term, but its intended positive effect generally does not last over a long period of time. Something else is needed. Affirmations become effective when an individual taps on the correct acupressure point.

It is not necessary for you to accept yourself about having the problem. This is true because you are making such a statement while simultaneously tapping the correct acupressure point. My recommendation is to use the self-acceptance statements previously given to eliminate the Psychological Reversals. However, you can use the following phrases instead.

For the Massive Reversal you could say:

"Like all people I have problems and limitations."

For the Specific Reversal you could say:

"Even though I have this problem it is difficult and I have been trying my best." or

"This is a difficult problem. If it was easy, I would have overcome it by now."

For the Future Reversal you could say:

"This problem is difficult and it might continue for a while."

"I may only may be able to improve some but not completely."

Remember to say the phrase you choose three times while you simultaneously verbalize your affirmation.

Chart of Tapping Points

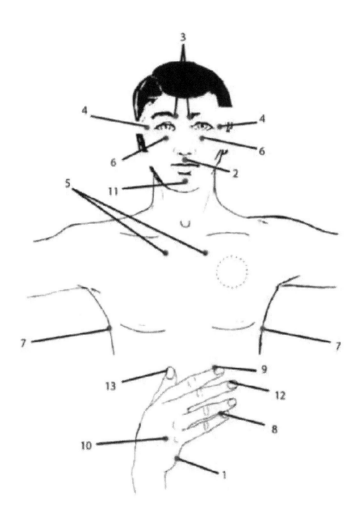

Figure 1 shows you which acupressure points are tapped in Peak Performance Optimization.

Description of the Location of the Acupressure Points:

Most of the time you are to tap with the tips of the index and middle finger.

Acupressure point 1 = Tap with two fingertips on the side of the other hand. The spot is exactly what is used when someone is making a karate chop. Do not tap on your wrist.

Acupressure point 2 = Tap with two fingertips directly under the middle of your nose.

Acupressure point 3 = Tap with two fingertips the inside of your eyebrow. You are tapping on the hairs near the center of your face.

Acupressure point 4 = Tap with two fingertips the bone directly to the outside corner of the eye.

Acupressure point 5 = You will use your entire hand. Put your hand in the shape of a V. Tap directly under your throat with your thumb on one side and all four fingers on the other side. You tap this way instead of with two fingers to make it easier to stimulate this particular acupressure point.

Acupressure point 6 = Tap with two fingertips on the bone directly under the middle of one of your eyes.

Acupressure point 7 = Tap with your entire hand on the other side of your body at breast level. You tap this way instead of with two fingers to make it easier to stimulate this particular acupressure point.

Acupressure point 8 = Tap with two fingertips on the inside cuticle (closest to your thumb) on the pinky of the other hand. Thus, you are tapping where the nail meets the skin.

Acupressure point 9 = Tap with two fingertips on the inside cuticle of the index finger on the other hand. Thus, you are tapping where the nail meets the skin.

You tap seven times for each of acupressure points 1 through 9.

Acupressure point 10 = Is located in the area between the area of the knuckles for the fourth and fifth finger. It is like a gutter in a bowling alley. Move two fingertips of the other hand back and forth in this gutter. You must make sure that your fingertips are on this gutter that is closest to the outside of your hand. Notice the lowest point. You tap with 2 fingertips of one hand on the lowest point in this gap on the other hand.

Acupressure point 10 is tapped about 30 times. This is because it has a number of positive effects that the other acupressure points do not have.

After doing PPO a few times there is no need to time yourself or count the number of times, you tap on acupressure point 10. You simply tap for a while and notice what thoughts come into your head and how your feelings change.

Comprehensive Acupressure Tapping Sequence (CATS): There are times when you feel bad but do not know what specific emotion you are feeling. There are just negative body sensations.

The Comprehensive Acupressure Tapping Sequence Points are tapped in the following order:

3-4-5-6-7-5-8-9-2-11-5-10-5.

I have never had a client that needed to tap acupressure points 12 and 13 to improve in the mental aspects of tennis.

The 10th acupressure point is tapped 30 times. It is best to just tap this point numerous times and notice what thoughts come to mind and how your feelings and body sensations may be changing.

Write down your Distress Rating.

Apply CATS again.

You can see a video of the Comprehensive Acupressure Tapping Sequence (CATS) by going to:

Book.PerformAtPeak.com and then click on **"Comprehensive Acupressure Tapping Sequence (CATS)".**

The Brain Balance Procedure: This nine-step procedure integrates the positive changes and shifts that are occurring during PPO. Clients understandably find this one of the strangest procedures, but it is effective. Specific steps stimulate different regions of the brain. Distress Ratings further decrease during this technique.

To stimulate the occipital lobe, located in the back of your brain, you will do eye movements. While doing them, imagine that you are looking at a clock that is facing you, with 3:00 to your right and 9:00 to your left. After doing the eye movements you will stimulate the right hemisphere of the brain by humming different notes. You count from one to five to stimulate the left hemisphere.

While you continuously tap on the 10th acupressure point, the procedure is done the following way:

1) Close your eyes.
2) Open your eyes and look straight ahead.
3) Move your eyes to 5:00 on the clock.
4) Move your eyes to 7:00 on the clock.
5) Circle your eyes clockwise for two revolutions.
6) Circle your eyes counterclockwise two revolutions.

7) Hum high and low notes without words.

8) Count to five, preferably out loud.

9) Hum high and low notes.

You can see a video of the Brain Balance Procedure by going to:

Book.PerformAtPeak.com, and then click on **"Brain Balance Procedure"**.

You then apply CATS again.

One Tapping Round of PPO: Since you eliminated the Psychological Reversals and did CATS two different times (Steps 2 and 4) and did the Brain Balance Procedure (Step 3), you will have completed one Tapping 'Round of PPO.

You can see a video of a round of PPO by going to:

Book.PerformAtPeak.com, and then click on **"One Round of PPO"**.

If your Distress Rating is not zero when doing PPO, notice what emotion you feel. If it is the same exact emotion, then repeat the round that you just completed two more times.

It is also possible that you will experience a different emotion. Recall that a change of an emotion may be just a different aspect of the problem. If so, just repeat three tapping rounds to decrease the new negative emotion.

If you feel differently, but are unable to label it or unsure, just do CATS.

Do a total of three rounds even if the type of emotion that you felt after any round changed.

If your Distress Rating is now 1 or 2, do the Eye Roll Procedure. The goal of any session is to eliminate all distress i.e., your Distress

Rating is 0.

If you are doing PPO about future performance and not getting your Distress Rating to 1 or less, you should follow the steps of using the Past Perspective Protocol for past upsetting experiences. As you identify those experiences and significantly lower or eliminate the distress from these past times, you could then reapply PPO when thinking about and picturing having your problem interfere with how well you are playing in a future match.

If you are not at a 1 or less, go back later that day or in two days and think of the problem. Whether you have the same feeling that you originally had does not matter. Simply do a PPO session. If you still cannot get your Distress Rating to 1 or less, the Troubleshooting Chapter will provide a guide of how you will get better results.

Practice Makes Perfect In PPO

If you do PPO repeatedly for different problems with the mental aspects of tennis, you can find that the application of PPO is not difficult and can take under 10 minutes. It will take more applications of PPO over different days to help more complex problems.

To facilitate your learning of PPO, a number of examples of tennis players improving the mental and physical aspects of their games are provided. Each story is followed by an analysis of the "Lessons to be Learned."

His Serve Improved Without Reliving Past Upsetting Experiences

Patrick D was a 31-year-old banker who wanted to improve his play at the end of matches, especially when serving. He had a history of playing too conservatively on important points. Pat would miss his first serves, become timid, and double-faulted too often. To activate the problem, I asked him to think about and picture himself serving at 5-4 or 6-5 in the third and deciding set. He did not experience any negative feelings. I then asked him to think about this scenario as he was competing against the player he was dying to beat, but never had. I have labeled such players "arch enemies." This got to Pat and he reported feeling nervous and tense. It was fortuitous that he was playing his opponent in two days. Patrick felt apprehensive and rated the intensity of his negative feeling as an 8. This then is his Distress Rating before applying a tapping round.

After tapping to eliminate the Psychological Reversals, he then did Step 2 by applying CATS. His distress reduced to a 6. The Brain Balance Procedure reduced his nervousness to a 4. He then did CATS and gave a Distress Rating of 3. Because his Distress Rating was higher than 2, the Eye Roll Procedure was not done. He did a second Tapping Round.

After the second round, he reported having a "twinge of nervousness," which was rated as a 1. Although he felt much less nervous, the goal in all sessions is to eliminate all negative feelings. So he followed with the Eye Roll Procedure, and he no longer felt any distress. Although done with the PPO session, there are more benefits that he can derive.

Another goal in PPO is to inoculate you against your weakness as much as possible. To do that, add elements to how you might have to face this problem in the future. This usually leads to a greater generalization of improving your skills. To facilitate inoculation against this problem so that the positive effects of this exercise would be maximized, I had Patrick think about different scenarios when serving with the lead. This included serving when at match point, when up 40-15 and down 15-40. I also had him picture these scenarios when playing against different opponents. Varying degrees of distress were elicited and then eliminated.

During the rounds, he realized that he focused too much on where to place his serve and needed to trust his first thoughts of where to serve and how to play the points.

Patrick called me about seven weeks later and told me the sessions were very helpful. He had been serving and winning the closing sets more often, rarely double-faulted in the last service game and was feeling more relaxed. He also reported that his return of serve seemed to be better. This had never been focused on in our sessions and, yet, this part of his game improved.

Lessons to Learn: Initially, Patrick did not have any negative feelings. The first thing done was getting him to add a component to his projection of playing in the future. He did that by thinking about playing his friend who he had never beaten. Fortunately, Patrick was playing him in the near future. Knowing that the competition is coming soon generally increases the intensity of negative feelings, such as apprehension and anxiety, and body sensations, such as tightness and tension. This had that exact effect on him.

The correct acupressure points were tapped as well as the Brain Balance Procedure. All negative feelings were eliminated after two rounds of PPO and after using the Eye Roll procedure. To improve his serve under different circumstances, he thought about serving at the end of the match, even when the circumstances of different scores were added. Each time his Distress Rating went to zero after doing Tapping Rounds of acupressure point sequences. Patrick developed better insight into how he could play better by utilizing different strategies. Not only had the goal of serving better at the end of a match been achieved, but his return of serve also improved even though this was never focused on in the PPO sessions. This is an example of the Generalization Effect. Lastly, Patrick did not have to activate past upsetting experiences because all distress was removed when taking a Future Perspective.

Needing to Work on Past Upsetting Experiences

Sometimes applying PPO for future playing does not help enough or at all. That's when past upsetting experiences about the problem need to be worked on.

If this occurs, it is necessary to follow guidelines specified in the Past Perspective Protocol. In summary, the worst upsetting experience(s) of when your problem in tennis occurred are identified and activated. After PPO significantly lowers or eliminates the Distress Ratings, the Future Perspective is applied. You can try to project playing into the future and that your weakness is causing you to play poorly. Having reduced the negative feelings from the past upsetting experiences, Distress Ratings will then come down more easily in a PPO session when taking a Future Perspective. The probability increases of then eliminating your problem when playing.

Kenny P. was a 15-year-old who started to play tennis three years earlier. His parents were members of a country club where he received instruction. Kenny quickly developed his tennis game. He continued to benefit from taking more lessons from other instructors. He played regularly and made his high school team. However, he hit a point when lessons were not helping, and his game plateaued. Kenny was not consistent from the baseline and was especially having trouble with his backhand in singles and doubles.

Kenny was leery about working with me; it was his parents' idea. He was slow to answer my questions and usually responded with one sentence and sometimes just one word. I asked if he was familiar with the mental aspects of tennis. I recommended that he go on amazon.com and do a search on "tennis mental game," and he got numerous hits. I did not tell him to read the books, as I was pretty sure he would not do so and did not want to give him instructions that he would not follow.

We discussed his problem in tennis. In the first session I also asked a number of questions to get an idea of his personality and academic and social life. In our second session, he informed me that he was surprised about how many books there were on the mental game in tennis. He also told me that he went on my web site, **PerformAtPeak.com**, and found the information "weird." I agreed that it was and also pointed out that he was taking numerous lessons and not improving. I reminded him that in the first session he discussed being frustrated with himself because his game was not improving.

He had taken additional lessons for two weeks while participating in the school team's practices. He was still having the same problems. An old pattern of losing matches occurred. At the end of the games determining the winner of the set and match, he had many unforced errors from the baseline on his forehand and backhand. When he started to make a few unforced errors, he also reported that he was tense and impatient. He was not successful when he tried to hit too many winners.

I asked Kenny to think about the last few matches that were most upsetting. He told me of a different doubles match where he played poorly and cost his high school team to lose. He felt frustrated and rated its intensity as an 8.

He did three Tapping Rounds. However, his Distress Rating only went down to a 5. This told me that there were probably other past experiences interfering with his progress.

I asked him to think about another upsetting experience, and he told me about a high school match that his parents and girlfriend attended. He recalled being nervous during that match. Just because he was nervous then did not mean I would ask him for a Distress Rating of that emotion. What counts is what he was feeling at the moment in our session when recalling that negative experience. He was feeling embarrassed that he played so poorly in front of his parents. The next Tapping Rounds decreased this feeling of embarrassment, but a feeling of disappointment came to the fore. Thus, the goal was to then decrease this negative feeling state. Two rounds using this CATS eliminated his distress.

It is always necessary to go back to the first emotion you had about the first memory you had when thinking about the problem. I asked Kenny to think of the match that caused his high school team to lose. This time he reported that his feeling of frustration was 2. He then did three tapping rounds. This feeling went away even though he was asked to focus on his experience of "blowing the match" that caused his school to lose.

I subsequently learned from his school coach that Kenny's game had elevated after a few lessons that enabled him to play better from the baseline during matches. He was less tense and feeling more confident. Kenny was making better decisions in his shot selection at the end of matches, enabling him to win more. He also was improving from his lessons from the same pros he worked with earlier. Within three weeks from the end of our sessions, he moved up from second doubles to third singles and then was winning the majority of his matches.

Lessons to Learn: This example points out that a problem has different causes from the past. Although he was young and had not been playing that long, Kenny was quite upset and it was obvious that using the Future Perspective Protocol would not be sufficient to fully decrease the effects of the past disturbing experiences. More than one upsetting experience had to be treated. He experienced more than one upsetting feeling. As such, he had to do more tapping rounds for each of these experiences. This can occur when initially applying the procedure, interrupted by a past memory that induces other feelings. It is more complicated when more than one upsetting experience comes to mind, but the problem can be resolved by following the steps of PPO when different emotions are experienced. Whenever different experiences are treated, go back to the original experience selected. Even though he had reached a period of time when lessons were not helping him, he started to benefit from them. We see that he not only feels better, but that he took a smarter approach of how to play at the end of a match.

When Emotions Cannot be Identified

There can be times when you do not know what emotion you are experiencing when you think about your weakness in tennis. Some people are not in touch with their feelings. They can tell that they do not feel good, but do not have a word to describe it. There may be a vague sense of "feeling bad." The actual emotion that might be occurring might be anger, depression or apprehension, but certain individuals do not know how to describe it. Distress Ratings are given about the intensity of the feeling. Even without a label for the emotions, it is not difficult to give a number to rate the intensity of the negative feeling. Sometimes the inability to identify emotions interferes with how much improvement can be made, but weaknesses have been greatly reduced or eliminated when using CATS.

Eddie F was a 36-year-old man who took up tennis about one year earlier. He had been an excellent athlete who played cornerback in football on a Division III college team. He was not good enough to play in professional leagues and started playing basketball. However, after about 10 years, he was getting injured too frequently, repeatedly twisting his ankles. After aggravating an old knee injury from playing football, he required arthroscopic surgery. He healed nicely from this. Since he continued to experience reoccurring physical problems, Eddie gave up basketball and started playing tennis and joined a tennis club.

Eddie took lessons and his game developed. He had kept in shape, was naturally fleet of foot and had good hand-eye coordination.

However, Eddie's game plateaued for over half a year. More frequent lessons did not help. He tried working with different instructors. He became unsure how to hit certain strokes because his instructors were telling him different ways to hit his forehand and backhand. None of this helped and he became increasingly frustrated with himself. He was very critical of how he was playing and became increasingly angry on the court. The game initially came easy to him, but not now. He was not playing as well as he had months ago.

We first dealt with how he couldn't understand why he was "hitting a brick wall." Eddie had difficulties identifying his feelings. He only had two in-person sessions with me and we later did two sessions on the internet. He then learned to do PPO by himself. I called him three months later to see how he was doing. Eddie had used PPO for his problem and reported that he just kept using the CATS every time. He liked the simplicity of it and was pleased with the results. He had decided to take lessons from one instructor and just worked on what he was being taught. He was playing better and was back to enjoying tennis.

Lessons to Learn: It is not necessary to label the disturbing emotion. Ratings were given about what he feels. We once again see the pattern of players choosing to work with one instructor.

Now that you've learned the major concepts, procedures and sequence of a PPO session, you are ready to apply it to yourself. PPO's main power lies in helping you with the psychological thought processes and emotional reactions. As they improve, you are on your way to performing at your peak.

CHAPTER 7

READY, SET AND GO: MAKE IT HAPPEN

I t is now time to apply Peak Performance Optimization (PPO) to substantially reduce or eliminate your biggest problems in tennis. Since this method is new and different, you will need to apply PPO a few times to sufficiently get accustomed to it in order to derive the maximum benefits.

When you are more proficient at doing PPO, the best times to do this procedure are:

Before a match. The closer in time that you do PPO the more likely it is to be effective.

After a match where you did not play well and are upset about it.

Before taking lessons.

You can apply PPO days before a match and it still be effective.

I recommend that you make photocopies of appendix 1 and 2. There are step by step procedures and tables to fill out your answers.

As PPO continues to help you, you can utilize the copied forms to use this method to continue to improve your tennis.

You previously read about the importance of deciding to use PPO using a past or future perspective.

The tables in this chapter will guide you throughout the application of PPO.

For now, think about the following:

Think about the main problem you are having in tennis that you want to decrease.

Think about your most important matches in the past. How much did your problem interfere with how well you played and in the outcome of the match?

How important is it for you to reduce this problem?

How much has your problem decreased?

How much time have you devoted to trying to decrease this problem?

If you have paid for lessons or for clinics to decrease this problem, approximately how much money have you spent?

Apex Problem: Although it should go without saying that the improvement you experience would be attributed to doing the PPO procedure, the existence of an Apex Problem may cause you not to attribute your improvement to having done this method. The danger of the Apex Problem is that you may not pursue decreasing other problems by using this method in the future. This is one of the reasons that you're being asked to answer additional questions. You will have a more accurate appraisal of how helpful PPO was to reducing your problem.

There are three more reminders before beginning.

It will be a good idea to watch the videos as you initially go through your PPO session.

Figure 1 appears so that it will be easier for you to know what acupressure points to tap.

Chart of Tapping Points

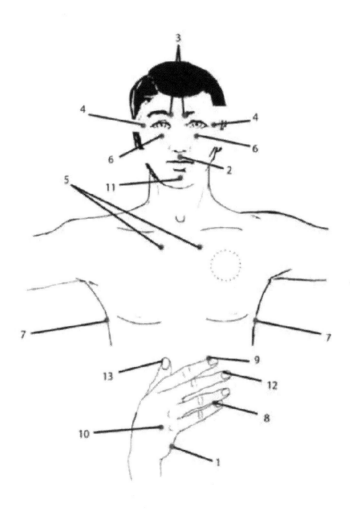

Figure 1 shows you which acupressure points are tapped in Peak
Performance Optimization.

Comprehensive Acupressure Tapping Sequence (CATS) This is the sequence of Acupressure Points that you tap for steps 2 and 4. The order of Acupressure Points tapped is:

3-4-5-6-7-5-8-9-2-11-5-10-5.

Each Acupressure Point is tapped about seven times, but the 10th is tapped 30 times. After getting used to this sequence, tap Acupressure Point 10 for a while and be aware of thoughts and feelings that come to your mind. You can write your answers on the tables in this chapter to get used to PPO. However, it is better to write down your answers on your photocopies the first time you are seriously doing Future and Past Protocols. You will be writing down Distress Ratings from 0-10 throughout these pages.

It is now time to start applying the PPO procedure.

Make a check mark of which perspective you will be taking to decrease your problem.

_____ Future Perspective Protocol   _____ Past Perspective Protocol

You can write your answers from photocopies of Appendix 1 and 2 or on the following pages.

If you are starting with the Future Perspective Protocol answers can be written on the next page.

If you are starting with the Past Perspective Protocol, go to page 96.

Use the QR to download appendices.

Applying PPO Using the Future Perspective Protocol

You can write your answers in the tables in this chapter, or you can go to appendix 1 and photocopy it. You will then have extra copies to use any time you want to apply PPO again.

Think about and picture your biggest problem in tennis. Think about playing an opponent you are competitive with. Imagine playing quite well and then all of a sudden your problem is occurring and you can't get it to stop. Then you start to make a number of different mistakes and are playing poorly. Keep in mind that this problem has been occurring and will occur in the future.

Greater activation of negative feelings will help PPO to more fully decrease your problem. You can picture this experience as a photograph, or see it occurring over time as you would with a video.

Describe this problem that you want to overcome.

_____

_____

_____

_____

_____

_____

Write the emotion or body sensations you are having right now at this moment. You are not too write down what you were feeling during that experience. What counts is the current feelings you are now experiencing.

_____

_____

_____

_____

How intense are you experiencing the negative emotion at this moment? Give a rating from 0-10.

Distress Rating = _____

1) Eliminate the three Psychological Reversals:

Tap on the karate spot (Acupressure Point 1) and say three times:

"I deeply and profoundly accept myself with all my problems and limitations."

Pause a few seconds. Tap on the karate spot on the other hand (Acupressure Point 1) and say three times:

"Even though I have this problem, I deeply accept myself."

Tap under your nose (Acupressure Point 2) and say three times:

"I deeply accept myself even if I never get completely over this problem."

Distress Rating = _____

(Recall that your Distress Rating may not go down from treating the reversals. This procedure removes the blocks that impede progress.)

2) Apply CATS by tapping on Acupressure Points:

3-4-5-6-7-5-8-9-2-11-5-10-5.

How intense are you experiencing the negative emotion at this moment? Give a rating from 0-10.

Distress Rating = _____

3) Brain Balance Procedure:

While you continuously tap on the 10th Acupressure Point, you are to simultaneously:

a) Close your eyes.
b) Open your eyes and look straight ahead.
c) Move your eyes to 5:00 on a clock by looking down to your right.
d) Move your eyes to 7:00 on a clock, by looking down to your left.
e) Circle your eyes clockwise for two revolutions.
f) Circle your eyes counterclockwise for two revolutions.
g) Hum high and low notes without words.
h) Count to 5 out loud.
i) Hum high and low notes.

How intense are you experiencing the negative emotion or body sensation at this moment? Give a rating from 0-10.

Distress Rating = _____

4) Apply CATS by tapping on Acupressure Points:

3-4-5-6-7-5-8-9-2-11-5-10-5.

How intense are you experiencing the negative emotion or body sensations at this moment? Give rating from 0-10.

Distress Rating = _____

If your Distress Rating is a 1 or 2, do the Eye Roll Procedure.

You have now completed one round of PPO for this negative emotion or body sensation. Even if your Distress Rating is zero, you still are to do three rounds.

You will now follow the same steps as you did in the first round.

Second Round

1) Eliminate the Specific Psychological Reversal:

Tap on the karate spot (Acupressure Point 1) and say three times:

"Even though I have this problem, I deeply accept myself."

Distress Rating = _____

2) Apply the CATS Procedure.

Distress Rating = _____

3) Do Brain Balance Procedure.

Distress Rating = _____

4) Apply the CATS Procedure

Distress Rating = _____

If the Distress Rating is a 1 or 2, apply the Eye Roll Procedure.

Distress Rating = _____

Even if your Distress Rating is zero, you still are to do the third round.

Third Round

1) Eliminate the Specific Psychological Reversal:

Tap on the karate spot (Acupressure Point 1) and say three times:

"Even though I have this problem, I deeply accept myself."

Distress Rating = _____

2 Apply the CATS Procedure

Distress Rating = _____

3) Do Brain Balance Procedure.

Distress Rating = _____

4) Apply the CATS Procedure.

Distress Rating = _____

If your Distress Rating is a 1 or 2, do the Eye Roll Procedure.

Important Assessment: If your Distress Rating is zero or a 1, then you are ready to go out to the court and play. Enjoy!

Guidelines on what to do when your Distress Rating is 2 or above:

Is your Distress Rating 2 or above? If you are still feeling the same emotion, apply the Past Perspective Protocol described below.

If your Distress Rating is 2 or above, notice if the emotion you are currently experiencing is different than what you felt when you started this Future Perspective Protocol. If you are feeling a different emotion, apply this Future Perspective Protocol for this new emotion. The same form that you wrote about using the Future Perspective Protocol is in Appendix 1

Once you have finished the three rounds of tapping for this new emotion what is your

Distress Rating = _____

If your Distress Rating is a zero or one, then you are ready to go out to the court and play. Enjoy!

If your Distress Rating is 2 or above, apply the Past Perspective Protocol that follows on the next page or use a photocopy of Appendix 2.

Applying the PPO Using the Past Perspective Protocol

You can write your answers below. You can go to appendix 2 and photocopy it. You will then have extra copies to use any time you want to apply PPO again.

Picture and think about the worst experience you had in the past when your problem occurred. Give yourself time to reflect on this memory. Try to remember it clearly as if it happened to you yesterday. Try to remember the most upsetting times in that entire experience. Keep doing so to activate a negative emotion or body sensation. Greater activation of negative feelings will help PPO to more fully decrease your problem. When thinking about this upsetting experience, you can picture it as a photograph or see it occurring over time as you would with a video.

Write about that experience:

_____
_____
_____
_____
_____
_____
_____

Write the emotion or body sensations you are having right now at this moment. You are not too write down what you were feeling during that experience. What counts is the current feelings you are now experiencing.

_____
_____
_____
_____

How intense are you experiencing the negative emotion at this moment? Give a rating from 0-10.

Distress Rating = _____

1) Eliminate the Psychological Reversals:

Tap on the karate spot (Acupressure Point 1) and say three times:

"I deeply and profoundly accept myself with all my problems and limitations."

Pause a few seconds. Tap on the karate spot on the other hand (Acupressure Point 1) and say three times:

"Even though I have this problem, I deeply accept myself."

Tap under your nose (Acupressure Point 2) and say three times:

"I deeply accept myself even if I never get completely over this problem."

Distress Rating = _____

(Recall that your Distress Rating may not go down from treating the reversals. This procedure removes the blocks that impede progress.)

2) Apply CATS by tapping on Acupressure Points:

3-4-5-6-7-5-8-9-2-11-5-10-5.

How intense are you experiencing the negative emotion at this moment? Give a rating from 0-10.

Distress Rating = _____

3) Brain Balance Procedure:

While you continuously tap on the 10th Acupressure Point, you are to simultaneously:

a) Close your eyes.
b) Open your eyes and look straight ahead.
c) Move your eyes to 5:00 on a clock by looking down to your right.
d) Move your eyes to 7:00 on a clock, by looking down to your left.
e) Circle your eyes clockwise for two revolutions.
f) Circle your eyes counterclockwise for two revolutions.
g) Hum high and low notes without words.
h) Count to 5 out loud.
i) Hum high and low notes.

How intense are you experiencing the negative emotion or body sensation at this moment? Give a rating from 0-10.

Distress Rating = _____

4) Apply CATS by tapping on Acupressure Points:

3-4-5-6-7-5-8-9-2-11-5-10-5.

How intense are you experiencing the negative emotion or body sensations at this moment? Give rating from 0-10.

Distress Rating = _____

If your Distress Rating is 2 or less, do the Eye Roll Procedure.

You have now completed one round of PPO for this negative emotion or body sensation. Even if your Distress Rating is zero, you still are to do three rounds.

You will now follow the same steps as you did in the first round.

Second Round

1) Eliminate the Specific Psychological Reversal:

Tap on the karate spot (Acupressure Point 1) and say three times:

"Even though I have this problem, I deeply accept myself."

Distress Rating = _____

2) Apply the CATS Procedure.

Distress Rating = _____

3) Do Brain Balance Procedure.

Distress Rating = _____

4) Apply the CATS Procedure

Distress Rating = _____

If the Distress Rating is a 1 or 2, apply the Eye Roll Procedure.

Distress Rating = _____

Even if your Distress Rating is zero, you still are to do the third round.

Third Round

1) Eliminate the Specific Psychological Reversal:

Tap on the karate spot (Acupressure Point 1) and say three times:

"Even though I have this problem, I deeply accept myself."

Distress Rating = _____

2 Apply the CATS Procedure

Distress Rating - _____

3) Do Brain Balance Procedure.

Distress Rating = _____

4) Apply the CATS Procedure.

Distress Rating = _____

If your Distress Rating is a 1 or 2, do the Eye Roll Procedure.

Important Assessment: If your Distress Rating using the past perspective is zero or 1, you will apply the Future Perspective Protocol. You can write your answers on the table below or on one your photocopies of the Future Perspective Protocol.

If your Distress Rating is not zero or 1 you will repeat the Past Procedure Protocol in reference to the second worst experience you had with the this problem. You can write your answers on one your photocopies of the Past Perspective Protocol in Appendix 2 or on the table that appears on page 107.

Applying the Future Perspective Protocol-Second Time

Once again think about and picture the problem you have in tennis that might occur in a future match. You will follow the same steps you did earlier when applying the Future Perspective Protocol. You will see the same instructions that you did the first time when you applied the Future Perspective Protocol. You may get the same emotions and body sensations that you did when you first applied the Future Perspective Protocol. However, you may have different emotions and body sensations.

You can write your answers in the tables in this chapter, or you can go to appendix 1 and photocopy it. You will then have extra copies to use any time you want to apply PPO again.

Think about and picture your biggest problem in tennis. Think about playing an opponent you are competitive with. Imagine playing quite well and then all of a sudden your problem is occurring and you can't get it to stop. Then you start to make a number of different mistakes and are playing poorly. Keep in mind that this problem has been occurring and will occur in the future.

Greater activation of negative feelings will help PPO to more fully decrease your problem. You can picture this experience as a photograph, or see it occurring over time as you would with a video.

Describe this problem that you want to overcome.

_____
_____
_____
_____
_____
_____

Write the emotion or body sensations you are having right now at this moment. You are not too write down what you were feeling during that experience. What counts is the current feelings you are now experiencing.

_____

_____

_____

_____

How intense are you experiencing the negative emotion at this moment? Give a rating from 0-10.

Distress Rating = _____

1) Eliminate the three Psychological Reversals:

Tap on the karate spot (Acupressure Point 1) and say three times:

"I deeply and profoundly accept myself with all my problems and limitations."

Pause a few seconds. Tap on the karate spot on the other hand (Acupressure Point 1) and say three times:

"Even though I have this problem, I deeply accept myself."

Tap under your nose (Acupressure Point 2) and say three times:

"I deeply accept myself even if I never get completely over this problem."

Distress Rating = _____

(Recall that your Distress Rating may not go down from treating the reversals. This procedure removes the blocks that impede progress.)

2) Apply CATS by tapping on Acupressure Points:

3-4-5-6-7-5-8-9-2-11-5-10-5.

How intense are you experiencing the negative emotion at this moment? Give a rating from 0-10.

Distress Rating = _____

3) Brain Balance Procedure:

While you continuously tap on the 10th Acupressure Point, you are to simultaneously:

a) Close your eyes.
b) Open your eyes and look straight ahead.
c) Move your eyes to 5:00 on a clock by looking down to your right.
d) Move your eyes to 7:00 on a clock, by looking down to your left.
e) Circle your eyes clockwise for two revolutions.
f) Circle your eyes counterclockwise for two revolutions.
g) Hum high and low notes without words.
h) Count to 5 out loud.
i) Hum high and low notes.

How intense are you experiencing the negative emotion or body sensation at this moment? Give a rating from 0-10.

Distress Rating = _____

4) Apply CATS by tapping on Acupressure Points:

3-4-5-6-7-5-8-9-2-11-5-10-5.

How intense are you experiencing the negative emotion or body sensations at this moment? Give rating from 0-10.

Distress Rating = _____

If your Distress Rating is a 1 or 2, do the Eye Roll Procedure.

You have now completed one round of PPO for this negative emotion or body sensation. Even if your Distress Rating is zero, you still are to do three rounds.

You will now follow the same steps as you did in the first round.

Second Round

1) Eliminate the Specific Psychological Reversal:

Tap on the karate spot (Acupressure Point 1) and say three times:

"Even though I have this problem, I deeply accept myself."

Distress Rating = _____

2) Apply the CATS Procedure.

Distress Rating = _____

3) Do Brain Balance Procedure.

Distress Rating = _____

4) Apply the CATS Procedure

Distress Rating = _____

If the Distress Rating is a 1 or 2, apply the Eye Roll Procedure.

Distress Rating = _____

Even if your Distress Rating is zero, you still are to do the third round.

Third Round

1) Eliminate the Specific Psychological Reversal:

Tap on the karate spot (Acupressure Point 1) and say three times:

"Even though I have this problem, I deeply accept myself."

Distress Rating = _____

2 Apply the CATS Procedure.

Distress Rating = _____

3) Do Brain Balance Procedure.

Distress Rating = _____

4) Apply the CATS Procedure.

Distress Rating = _____

If your Distress Rating is a 1 or 2, do the Eye Roll Procedure.

Important Assessment: If your Distress Rating is zero or a 1, then you are ready to go out to the court and play. Enjoy!

Guidelines on what to do when your Distress Rating is 2 or above:

Is your Distress Rating 2 or above? If you are still feeling the same emotion that you did at the start, apply the Past Perspective Protocol described back on page 96 or in Appendix 2.

If your Distress Rating is 2 or above, notice if the emotion you are currently experiencing is different than what you felt when you started this Future Perspective Protocol. If you are feeling a different emotion, apply this Future Perspective Protocol for this new emotion. The same form that you wrote about using the Future Perspective Protocol is in Appendix 1

Once you have finished the three rounds of tapping for this new emotion what is your

Distress Rating = _____

If your Distress Rating is a zero or one, then you are ready to go out to the court and play. Enjoy!

Is your Distress Rating 2 or above? If you are still feeling the same emotion, write your answers on the Past Perspective Protocol on the next page or on a photocopy of Appendix 2.

Applying the Past Perspective Protocol for the Second Worst Experience You Had In Tennis

The instructions below are similar to what you utilized the Past Perspective Protocol the first time you applied PPO to a past experience. You may have similar or different emotions that you had when you applied the Past Perspective Protocol the first time. You can write your answers below. You can go to appendix 2 and photocopy it. You will then have extra copies to use any time you want to apply PPO again.

Picture and think about the 2nd worst experience you had in the past when your problem occurred. Give yourself time to reflect on this memory. Try to remember it clearly as if it happened to you yesterday. Try to remember the most upsetting times in that entire experience. Keep doing so to activate a negative emotion or body sensation. Greater activation of negative feelings will help PPO to more fully decrease your problem. When thinking about this upsetting experience, you can picture it as a photograph or see it occurring over time as you would with a video.

Write down about that experience:

_____

_____

_____

_____

_____

_____

_____

_____

_____

_____

Write the emotion or body sensations you are having right now at this moment. You are not too write down what you were feeling during that experience. What counts is the current feelings you are now experiencing.

_____

_____

_____

_____

How intense are you experiencing the negative emotion at this moment? Give a rating from 0-10.

Distress Rating = _____

1) Eliminate the Psychological Reversals:

Tap on the karate spot (Acupressure Point 1) and say three times:

"I deeply and profoundly accept myself with all my problems and limitations."

Pause a few seconds. Tap on the karate spot on the other hand (Acupressure Point 1) and say three times:

"Even though I have this problem, I deeply accept myself."

Tap under your nose (Acupressure Point 2) and say three times:

"I deeply accept myself even if I never get completely over this problem."

Distress Rating = _____

(Recall that your Distress Rating may not go down from treating the reversals. This procedure removes the blocks that impede progress.)

2) Apply CATS by tapping on Acupressure Points:

3-4-5-6-7-5-8-9-2-11-5-10-5.

How intense are you experiencing the negative emotion at this moment? Give a rating from 0-10.

Distress Rating = _____

3) Brain Balance Procedure:

While you continuously tap on the 10th Acupressure Point, you are to simultaneously:

a) Close your eyes.
b) Open your eyes and look straight ahead.
c) Move your eyes to 5:00 on a clock by looking down to your right.
d) Move your eyes to 7:00 on a clock, by looking down to your left.
e) Circle your eyes clockwise for two revolutions.
f) Circle your eyes counterclockwise for two revolutions.
g) Hum high and low notes without words.
h) Count to 5 out loud.
i) Hum high and low notes.

How intense are you experiencing the negative emotion or body sensation at this moment? Give a rating from 0-10.

Distress Rating = _____

4) Apply CATS by tapping on Acupressure Points:

3-4-5-6-7-5-8-9-2-11-5-10-5.

How intense are you experiencing the negative emotion or body sensations at this moment? Give rating from 0-10.

Distress Rating = _____

If your Distress Rating is 1 or 2 do the Eye Roll Procedure.

You have now completed one round of PPO for this negative emotion or body sensation. Even if your Distress Rating is zero, you still are to do three rounds.

You will now follow the same steps as you did in the first round.

Second Round

1) Eliminate the Specific Psychological Reversal:

Tap on the karate spot (Acupressure Point 1) and say three times:

"Even though I have this problem, I deeply accept myself."

Distress Rating = _____

2) Apply the CATS Procedure.

Distress Rating = _____

3) Do Brain Balance Procedure.

Distress Rating = _____

4) Apply the CATS Procedure

Distress Rating = _____

If the Distress Rating is a 1 or 2, apply the Eye Roll Procedure.

Distress Rating = _____

Even if your Distress Rating is zero, you still are to do the third round.

Third Round

1) Eliminate the Specific Psychological Reversal:

Tap on the karate spot (Acupressure Point 1) and say three times:

"Even though I have this problem, I deeply accept myself."

   Distress Rating = _____

2) Apply the CATS Procedure

   Distress Rating - _____

3) Do Brain Balance Procedure.

   Distress Rating = _____

4) Apply the CATS Procedure.

   Distress Rating = _____

If your Distress Rating is a 1 or 2, do the Eye Roll Procedure.

Important Assessment: If your Distress Rating using the past perspective is zero or 1, you will apply the Future Perspective Protocol. You can write your answers on the table below or on one your photocopies of the Future Perspective Protocol.

If your Distress Rating is not zero or 1, you still should go out and play tennis. Applying the PPO procedure a number of times will still probably help your problem to decrease

It is also recommended if your negative psychological reactions have decreased some or not at all when you went out to play tennis after applying PPO, you should immediately apply PPO using the Past Perspective Protocol about your feelings when you think of this recent match. The intensity of these feelings will be greater the sooner you apply PPO after a match. This makes it more likely that you will derive better results from following these methods. Do this after any match where your problem may have reemerged or for other weaknesses in your game that you want to improve.

If your problems persist the information in the next chapter will be helpful. You may simply have to modify the PPO procedure. Your application of these procedures makes it easier for you to decrease the problem that you have identified.

"We are made to persist. That's how we find out who we are."

Tobias Wolff

CHAPTER 8

TROUBLESHOOTING AND REFINING PEAK PERFORMANCE OPTIMIZATION

This chapter is written for a number of reasons. You may have gotten the results you desired, but believe there is more to learn. Perhaps Peak Performance Optimization (PPO) has helped to decrease some but not all of the problems you have applied it on. Or, you have seen it has been helpful but are pretty sure that you can get even better results. If you have been working with someone else utilizing PPO, this chapter is helpful in that one of you may have greater insight into how PPO could work better for the other. And then, there are some who have gotten little benefit from PPO. Of those, even if you are frustrated and doubting that PPO could help you, stick it out a little longer as this chapter provides solutions. Even if you still doubt that PPO could help you, it is a good sign that you have begun to read this chapter. It is recommended that you read the entire chapter because you may need to follow more than one modification of PPO.

No one method works for everyone all of the time. Like all methods, there are subtleties that require refinements for better results for some individuals. Modifications of the PPO method are provided. However, you will also see explanations of the factors that necessitate changes in how you apply PPO. These explanations will give you better insight into this transformative process.

You know that your application of PPO has not gotten the maximal results when:

1) You are unable to get your Distress Ratings to very low figures, especially to 1 or less.
2) Distress Ratings have gone significantly down, even reaching zero, but your problem in your tennis game still persists.

PPO is an entirely new and quite different procedure. It does take time to learn how to apply it properly. Hopefully you have not rushed and have taken the steps one at a time. If not, you probably have not correctly followed the directions.

Although you have been given a significant amount of new information, recall that PPO has the following basic procedural structure:

You think about the problem and notice the negative feelings and their intensity. After giving a Distress Rating at the beginning and after each of the four following steps, you then:

1) Tap to eliminate the Psychological Reversals.
2) Tap the sequence of acupressure points that correspond to the negative feelings you are having (SQ).
3) Do the Brain Balance Procedure.
4) Repeat SQ.

Reasons why you did not get the Maximum Results from PPO

You did not do PPO correctly: Review the Self-Application chapter. Make sure you know how to correctly do each of the steps.

Do not immediately try to apply it again. Read through it first and think about it. You'll probably catch whatever error you were making. You probably should review the videos of the different techniques that can be seen at **Book.PerformAtPeak.com**.

You may have skipped an important step: Since PPO is a new and different method, you may simply need to have more practice. Think of how many times you have taken lessons or practiced to improve a stroke or serve. You probably need to repeat PPO a few more times.

Room was provided to write down your answers in chapter 7 and in the appendices. If you did not write down your responses on the tables in chapter 7, go back and use the work sheets from Appendix 1 and 2 when reapplying PPO.

The tables in Chapter 7 are slightly more specific in terms of when you might switch between the Past and Future Perspective Protocols. As such, it is recommended that you use the tables in Chapter 7 the first time you are doing PPO and getting used to how to apply it.

You may have difficulty identifying emotions and have tapped the wrong acupressure points. Since almost all of the tapping sequences for the different emotions are contained in the CATS, you may be better off just applying this tapping sequence for steps 2 and 4. Conversely, you may have applied CATS for steps 2 and 4 and need to do one of the shorter tapping sequences associated with a specific emotion. Try making that change.

Make sure you have correctly treated all three Psychological Reversals: You have to tap on the right acupressure point and verbalize the associated affirmation. Failure to remove this powerful force can preclude the lowering or elimination of distress in your session. The steps to follow to eliminate these reversals have been provided throughout the chapters.

Additional Psychological Reversals may Need to be Eliminated

Psychological Reversals block or severely limit the efficacy of PPO. A description and the treatment of Massive, Specific and Future Reversals have been given. However, there are two main thematic reversals that sometimes also need to be eliminated.

Deserve Reversal: The unconscious configuration of neural circuits may be such that there is a stronger force of believing one does not deserve to be over their problem. There may be a reason from your past that makes this reversal exist. If so, this is usually related to experiences of shame and guilt. You may not have done anything wrong, yet have to eliminate this obstruction. You simply eliminate this reversal by:

Tapping right under your lower lip (acupressure point 11) and verbalizing the following affirmation three times:

"I deeply accept myself even though I do not deserve to be over this problem."

Although this affirmation is difficult to say and may not make complete sense, tapping the correct acupressure point and verbalizing the affirmation is how you correct this Psychological Reversal.

Safety Reversal: The unconscious configuration in your brain about your problem can be tied to feeling it's not safe to be over this problem. The most common example of this is a child feeling uneasy and nervous when starting to defeat a parent or older sibling. However, there does not have to be any reason from the past of why this reversal has to be in your life now. You simply have to eliminate this reversal by:

Tapping under your nose (acupressure point 2) and verbalizing the following affirmation three times:

"I deeply accept myself even though it is not safe to be over this problem."

Modification of the PPO procedure: Activate the problem and note your Distress Rating. After doing the tapping and affirmation to eliminate the Massive, Specific and Future Reversals, add the treatments for the Deserve and Safety Reversals that you just read.

1) Tap to eliminate all 5 Psychological Reversals.
2) Apply CATS or tap on the acupressure points associated with that emotion.
3) Do the Brain Balancing Procedure.
4) Tap on the same acupressure points tapped in step 3.

Continue to do three of these tapping rounds and follow all other guidelines that you have been given.

Belief Ratings: You could be following the correct steps of thinking about and picturing the problem in order to activate the weakness in your tennis game, but simply do not have or notice any negative emotions or body sensations at such times.

However, with any repetitive problem, there are invariably negative beliefs or thoughts. Such thoughts or beliefs could be about difficulties you have with certain parts of tennis.

"I just can't hit a slice serve."

"Serve and volleying are too difficult."

"Learning to hit topspin off my backhand is way too hard."

Other negative and harsh beliefs are more problematic because they are about being deficient in some way. Examples could include:

"I am and will continue to be a nervous wreck."

"I just will never be good at the sport."

"I suck."

Modification of PPO procedure: You can still apply PPO by giving Belief Ratings. The rating is on how true you think that negative belief is. The rating is from 0-10, where 10 reflects that you think your belief is absolutely true. Zero would reflect that you no longer think that your original belief is correct.

You then apply the exact same PPO procedures. The only difference is that you will be giving a Belief Rating instead of the Distress Rating. Your thoughts will change as you do this method. Most people who start a Tapping Round eventually start feeling some negative emotions or body sensations. When that occurs, go back to the original protocol, where you are making Distress Ratings about your negative feelings. You keep applying PPO until you have little or no distress. At that point, go back and give a rating about the original negative belief. If the Belief Rating is 2 or above, repeat the same PPO procedure. I will warn you that it is difficult to get the Belief and Distress Ratings in such cases to zero when it is difficult for you to have or notice your negative emotions or body sensations. However, decreases in the Belief Rating will help how you react on the tennis court

Example of a Belief Rating: Harold thought about his poor play at the end of a match. When thinking about it, he did not have any negative feelings. However, he labeled himself a "choker." He was then asked to rate:

"How true is it that you are a choker?"

His belief that this was true was rated as a 7 on a 0 -10 scale. Once starting PPO he became aware of being angry with himself. Notice that he went from not feeling any emotions to now feeing angry. Thus, ratings then became of how intense he was currently feeling at this moment in the session. He then gave this a Distress Rating of 8. Tapping Rounds were done and his distress went to a 2. It is necessary to go back and give a Belief Rating to the original question. He rated this as a 3 when once again being asked "How true is it that you are a choker?" He was satisfied with the results, but it would have been better if all ratings were zero.

There is an important point that applies to certain people. This occurs when a person deeply pushes down their negative feelings. As such, one would apply PPO with Belief Ratings. Pushing down negative feelings is known as suppression. PPO always moves you towards health. For such individuals, negative feelings can emerge such that you are now experiencing greater distress than previously. This is simply a step on the path of moving towards being in a better psychological state. Just simply apply PPO and those negative feelings will reduce.

Tapping Specific Acupressure Points: Sometimes PPO will not be completely effective. For some people, better outcomes occur when a more concise and specific tapping sequence is used in place of CATS in steps 2 and 4. The table below specifies which acupressure point tapping sequences are associated with each of the disturbing emotion that most often comes up in tennis:

Emotion:	Acupressure points
Anxiety-Nervousness:	6-7-5-10-5
Apprehension:	2-6-7-5-10-5
Frustration-Rage:	4-5-10-5
Embarrassment:	2-5-10-5
Discouraged-Feeling Down-Defeated:	10-5 or 4-5-10-5.
Shame:	11-5-10-5

For example, CATS is usually applied in PPO. However, it may not be that helpful and a more specific acupressure tapping sequence is needed. If your problem involves being too nervous at the end of a close match, you would tap acupressure points 6-7-5-10-5 instead of all the acupressure points tapped in CATS. If you get too angry and upset, you would tap acupressure points 4-5-10-5. Figure 1 is provided to make it easier for you to know which acupressure points are to be tapped with any specific negative emotion.

Chart of Tapping Points

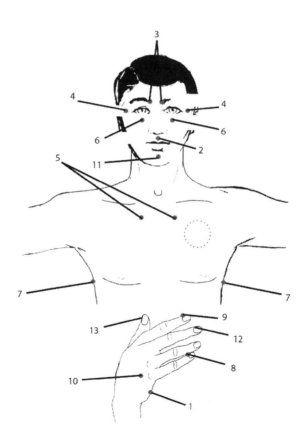

Figure 1 shows you which acupressure points are tapped in Peak Performance Optimization.

When writing your answers on appendix 1 or 2, or on the tables provided in the book, write these tapping sequences so that you will apply them as opposed to doing CATS. The necessity of treating specific acupressure points does not come up often if all other aspects of PPO are applied correctly. However, be aware that this is one step that may have to be applied to get optimal results.

Energetic Disorganization: This is a generalized state of being characterized by disturbances in thought processes, learning and behavior. It affects biological, neurological and energetic processes. Normal biological or metabolic processes cannot exist when in this psychological state. The first substantial work in this area was done by David Walther in his text on Applied Kinesiology, relating it to problems in the cranial-sacral primary respiratory mechanism. He referred to this as "Neurological Disorganization". However, this is too severe of a term. Since we are working with the acupressure energetic system, the term "Energetic Disorganization" is more appropriate.

Difficulties controlling emotions such as anxiety and anger, and even getting overexcited, characterize and can elicit this energetic disturbance or, in effect, be a consequence of this obstructive force. There are a number of examples in everyday life that reflect this energetic disorganization. These would include saying words in the wrong order a sentence, reversing letters when spelling, clumsiness, and confused behavior—i.e., putting silverware in the refrigerator while putting a small container of milk in the dishwasher. It's a deterioration in concentration and memory or being in what feels like a fog. Energetic disturbance is theorized to contribute to attention deficit disorder and dyslexia.

Examples of energetic disorganization in tennis are mixing up the scores (calling the returner's number first and the server's second), forgetting who is to serve, not recognizing to switch sides at the appropriate time and walking to serve in the deuce court when it should be the ad court or vice versa.

Simplified Collarbone Breathing Procedure: The easiest way to get rid of such an energetic disorganization is to do a method known as "Simplified Collarbone Breathing." This is another procedure that will seem strange. Once again, I would instruct you to simply follow the directions by going to:

Book.PerformAtPeak.com, and then click on **"Simplified Collarbone Breathing"**

The collarbone meridian (acupressure point 5) is the only acupressure point stimulated when doing this method. When you tapped this acupressure point during the PPO procedure, you used one hand to tap on it to make it easy to tap. However, for the Simplified Collarbone Breathing Procedure, you need to put the fingertips of your index and middle fingers near the exact collarbone acupressure point.

You find the collarbone acupressure point in the following way: Place the fingertips of your right index and middle finger in the sternal notch, which is located at the gap at the bottom of your throat. Slowly move the two fingertips down 1 inch. Then slowly move these two fingertips 1 inch to the left. Then you take the fingertips of the left index and middle fingers in the sternal notch. Slowly move the two fingertips down 1 inch. Then slowly move these two fingertips 1 inch to the right. You may think you are in the correct place because you are between tiny bone-like structures. However, this does not guarantee that you are at the correct location. To get more adept at finding the collarbone acupressure point, I recommend that you use a mirror to make sure you are moving the fingertips 1 inch down and then 1 inch to the side. Your placement does not have to be perfect, but it is necessary to get the fingertips near this location. In the beginning, it is best to find this acupressure point by looking in a mirror when you are moving your fingers. Figure 1 shows the placement of the fingertips. Note that your hands are crossing at the wrist.

Figure 1: Placement of Fingertips for Simplified Collarbone Breathing

Figure 2: Placement of Knuckles for Simplified Collarbone Breathing

Once your fingertips are in the correct position, follow this breathing sequence:

1) Breathe normally, one full respiration in and out; one full breath in and out.
2) Take a full breath in, then take another breath in and hold it.

3) Let out about halfway and hold for 2 seconds.
4) Let all the breath out two or three times through the mouth and hold for 2 seconds.
5) Take a half breath in and hold for 2 seconds.

You are halfway through this simplified version of Collarbone Breathing Procedure. See Figure 2 for the positioning of the fist.

Instead of your fingertips being on the collarbone point, place your knuckles on the acupressure point 5. This is done by removing your fingertips from the collarbone acupressure point, opening your hand, bending your thumb inside into the palm of your hand and making a fist by closing your fingers over your thumb. Put the knuckles of the right index and middle fingers on the left collarbone point while your hand remains in a fist. Put the knuckles of the left index and middle fingers on the right collarbone point while your hand remains in a fist. Figure 2 shows the positioning of the fist and knuckles. You will then apply the same five-step breathing sequence described above.

Although this procedure does not seem simple at first, you very well may be able to complete it in under 40 seconds after doing this a few times.

Modification of the PPO procedure: Apply the Simplified Collarbone Breathing procedure before treating the Psychological Reversals

Thus, a round of PPO would involve:

1) Apply the Simplified Collarbone Breathing Technique,
2) Tap to eliminate the Psychological Reversals
3) Apply CATS or tap on the acupressure points associated with that emotion,
4) Do the Brain Balancing Procedure,
5) Tap on the same acupressure points tapped in step 3.

Continue to do three of these tapping rounds and follow all other guidelines that you have been given.

Hypersensitivities: These are substances that interfere with how much PPO can help. They can also interfere with how one plays. Hypersensitivities are usually detected by using Applied Kinesiology. Recall that during this method one arm is put to the side at shoulder length by the subject. The tester then pushes down on the subject's extended arm with the same amount of force. The subject's muscle strength may vary depending on what is said.

Detecting the presence of a hypersensitivity can occur in the following manner. The individual may say "Pure Water" and the tester pushes down on the subject's arm and it does not budge. Let's say that that individual smoke cigarettes and we are not absolutely certain that this is a hypersensitivity. The subject would then verbalize the word "cigarette". If it a hypersensitivity, the subject's arm would automatically weaken and go down even though the tester is not pushing the arm down with any greater force. In other words, hypersensitivities weaken one's muscles. Thus, it is not surprising that hypersensitive can impair performance. It is not just that the cigarettes make the player more tired, but that it is s a substance that quickly saps strength even when no running is occurring.

Hypersensitivities also limit or prevent PPO from helping. Even if you apply PPO correctly, the distress you experience in a PPO session may decrease very little. Your problems in tennis are not likely to improve if you cannot get your Distress Ratings low. Hypersensitivities cause an imbalance of the acupressure energy system. They can prevent treatments that eliminate Psychological Reversals to become ineffective.

Hypersensitivities have a negative effect through ingestion or as a noxious stimulus to the olfactory and kinesthetic sensory systems.

They occur by eating, drinking and having objects come in contact with your skin.

Applied Kinesiology is too complex for the reader to currently apply to detect hypersensitivities. You can learn this method at PerformAtPeak.com. However, there are basic strategies and methods that can be utilized. A useful guide is to suspect that the more chemical the substance, the more likely that it is a hypersensitivity. The most common hypersensitivities are:

1) Tobacco smoke
2) Perfume
3) Cologne
4) Hairspray
5) Aftershave
6) Scented shampoo
7) Scented conditioners or gels
8) Cell phone on you

Less obvious, but possible hypersensitivities include:

9) Food coloring
10) Artificial sweeteners
11) Spicy foods
12) Scented laundry detergents
13) Scented clothes softeners
14) Dry cleaned or new clothes

Even natural substances can be hypersensitivities. We see this in everyday life for some people who have an intolerance of dairy products. In the same manner, such grains as certain wheat, corn or soy products and large amounts of coffee can be impediments to the effectiveness of PPO. Keep in mind that some of the hypersensitivities are not necessarily unhealthy for you but do interfere with the effectiveness of PPO. For instance someone may have a lactose intolerance and drinking milk would likely interfere with the PPO's efficacy.

An ideal time to do PPO is in the morning before you eat, drink coffee or shower. Many people meditate when they first get up. You can do the same with PPO. You should have some water before you start, as some degree of dehydration can also interfere with the effectiveness of PPO.

Sometimes one cannot avoid a hypersensitivity. Fortunately, there is a method that temporarily neutralizes hypersensitivities without using Applied Kinesiology. This enables a tennis player to neutralize the obstruction that a hypersensitivity could cause and, with some practice, this method can be done quickly within a PPO session

Energy Neutralization Technique: Dr. Doris Rapp is a physician who was a pioneer in the field of Environmental Medicine. She learned and demonstrated a method, Frontal Occipital Holding that often eliminates the obstruction caused by hypersensitivities. You apply Frontal Occipital Holding by having one hand horizontally on your forehead, with your fingers touching each other. See Figure 3 for the placement of hands. The thumb does not touch the head at all. Your other hand is placed horizontally on the back of your head with all five fingers—they are on the back of the skull. Your thumb rests on the lowest part of your hard skull and not on your neck. You press both hands into your head with moderate pressure while inhaling and then stop pressing as you exhale. You do this three times. You then tap on acupressure point 1 and verbalize three times "_____(Substance) I do not want it to intefere with treatment." You then tap on acupressure point 2 and verbalize two times "_____(Substance)will not interfere with treatment." A more detailed description will make this clearer.

Cologne could be an example of this phenomenon. You would then do the Frontal Occipital Holding procedure three times. Then tap with two fingertips on acupressure point 1 and say three times, "Cologne I do not want it to interfere with treatment." Then tap on acupressure point 2 and say three times, "Cologne will not interfere with treatment." I know this procedure seems strange, but is similar to other methods in Holistic Medicine, Crainiosacral therapy and Energy Psychology. This is one more time to simply follow the instructions.

Figure 3: Placement of hands for Frontal Occipital Holding

To see a video of this procedure go to:

Book.PerformAtPeak.com, and then click on **"Energetic Neutralization Technique"**

Modification of the PPO procedure: If hypersensitivities are present when applying PPO, there is a chance that you will not get yourDistress and Belief Ratings to zero. Thus, it is important to have a strategy to limit interference by potential hypersensitivities.

As best you can try to avoid the substances listed above before applying PPO. It is best to do PPO first thing in the morning, even before taking a shower (soaps and shampoos may be hypersensitivities) or drinking coffee. Ideally, all you would need to do is drink water and then begin the PPO procedure.

However, many of my clients do PPO at some point before the match. Hypersensitivities are the number one because preventing the correction of Psychological Reversals, As such, it is recommended that you apply the hypersensitivity neutralization technique to 1-3 substances you suspect might be interfering. You are to apply the hypersensitivity neutralization technique before tapping to eliminate Psychological Reversals.

Thus, a PPO would involve:

1) Avoid possible hypersensitivities or do a neutralization technique.
2) Tap to eliminate the Psychological Reversals.
3) Apply CATS.
4) Do the Brain Balancing Procedure.
5) Apply CATS.

Continue to do three of these tapping rounds and follow all other guidelines that you have been given.

There are times when I am working with an athlete over the internet and need to complete PPO to quickly get their Distress Rating to zero. I use the Energy Neutralization technique to neutralize any potential hypersensitivities that I suspect may be present before tapping to eliminate Psychological Reversals. It takes very little time to apply these techniques and can result in a quicker effect.

Additional Factors that Can Limit PPO Effectiveness

Any method that can be so powerfully effective sometimes requires refinements or adding components. Solutions for these are provided:

Lack of Hydration: Some people are extremely sensitive, physiologically about hydration. Even if you think that this does not apply to you, it is a good idea to drink at least 3 ounces of water or juice before starting. Drinking caffeinated coffee does not provide sufficient hydration.

You Need to Know: There are times for some people where PPO did not help or help is much as they had hoped. It is not that PPO cannot help. The inability to get the Distress Rating low has become a signal that this problem is more complicated or serious than you first thought. Fortunately, this does not occur much at all. The better you get at applying PPO, the greater you will benefit.

PPO is Not Helping Enough: What if I am a Complicated Case?

If you think that all these complications or subtleties apply to you, do PPO in the following order:

1) Drink at least 3 ounces of water or juice.
2) Avoid hypersensitivities or apply a hypersensitivity neutralization technique.
3) Do the Simplified Collarbone Breathing procedure,
4) Do the treatment for the Deserve and Safety Psychological Reversals after doing the steps to eliminate the three major Psychological Reversals.
5) Tap on CATS or the acupressure associated with the negative emotion you are feeling.
6) Do the Brain Balancing Procedure.
7) Tap on the same acupressure points tapped in step 5.

Continue to do three of these tapping rounds and follow all other guidelines that you have been given.

Hypersensitivities can adversely affect the level of play of the greatest tennis professionals. This is even true with the current men's number one tennis player in the world

CHAPTER 9

NOVAK DJOKOVIC'S DISCOVERY AND BECOMING NUMBER ONE IN THE WORLD

We tend to think that the top tennis professionals as having a childhood without too much strife or trauma. This would then allow a child to focus on tennis with few distractions, learn from different instructors and continuously practice. However, this was not the case for Novak Djokovic.

NATO forces started bombing his hometown of Belgrade during the Bosnia War. He grew up at a time when sirens would sound informing the people that planes were coming and bombs would soon be dropped on their city. He and his family struggled with the helplessness of not being able to stop this brutality and not knowing if they would live to see the next day. Adding to his burden he felt responsible for taking care of his younger brothers. Airplanes flew dangerously low and detonated bombs throughout the night. His entire family would run from their home and ended up staying in his aunt's bomb shelter for seventy-eight straight nights.

He survived all this and eventually met Jelena Gencic, his first tennis coach. She recognized his immense talent and dedication.

She became very committed to helping him develop as a tennis player and young man. His early life was not just about tennis. She also taught him to have an open mind to art and music. Although this may seem irrelevant, it helped him to be broad-minded and develop tolerance for new ideas.

Success came quickly as an adolescent. He was the Triple European champion in singles, doubles and in team competition and also European champion for boys 16 years old or younger.Djokovic became the youngest player to be ranked in the top 20 in the ATP ratings and then number 3 in the rankings.

Although his achievements were outstanding, he stayed at number 3 forty-three consecutive weeks. He then won his first grand slam tournament in the Australian open. However, his ascendance essentially stopped. He was unable to defend his 2008 Australian Open Championship because his stamina failed him and caused him to stop playing in the tournament. He finally got to play his first US open and ended up collapsing on the court due to exhaustion. His physical ailments were mocked by a few of the top tennis players.

Djookovic's difficulties did not occur because a lack of dedication and commitment. He increased the intensity and hours practicing and conditioning. All aspects of training increased, His runs were longer and weight lifting more demanding. He changed coaches and even had nasal surgery, which helped him to breathe more freely. Djokovic moved his training facility to the Persian Gulf, hoping that the extremely hot temperatures would enhance his conditioning. He considered that the problems were psychological and started yoga and mediating. Nonetheless, he felt slow, easily winded, overweight and not mentally sharp.

Fortunately, Dr. Cetojevic watched him play and collapse on the court. As a nutritionist he thought that Djokavic might be suffering from food allergies. Eventually they met. To test if Djokovic had significant food allergies, Dr. Cetojevic used an Applied Kinesiology method to detect any problems with what Djokavic ate or drank. Dr. Cetojevic referred to his technique as Kinesiological Arm Testing. However, it is essentially the same procedure that was described earlier in the book. Although food allergies were not tested in the first video on Psychological Reversals, a demonstration of Applied Kinesiology can be described. When applying this method, Djokavic held his arm to the side and at shoulder level. Dr. Cetojevic pushed down on Djokovic's arm and it remained strong. However, when Djokovic held a slice of bread, the arm he extended at shoulder level became weak when Dr. Cetojevic pushed down with the same amount of force. To test this further Djokavic stayed away from any product that contained gluten and started to feel better physically and psychologically. When he ate a bagel, the gluten made him sick. After much discussion Djokovic came to understand that consuming gluten had a number of deleterious physical and mental effects and was responsible for his past problems in tennis.

This had a profound effect on Djokovic. This eventually led Djokovic to stop eating and drinking products containing gluten. He attributes much of his success to eliminating gluten from his diet. As described in his book "Serve to Win: The 14-Day Gluten-Free Plan for Physical and Mental Excellence.", consuming food containing gluten caused his past difficulties with concentration, stamina and impaired performance. Once on a gluten free diet he lost excess weight, became faster, more flexible and developed greater endurance.

To win the 2012 Australian Open it took 4 hour and 50 minutes to prevail. His victory in the finals against Rafa Nadal took 5 hours and 53 minutes. This was the longest match of any finals in Grand Slam history. There were no longer any questions about his endurance.

It took more than these physical changes to catapult him to be the number one men's tennis player in the world. He reported that excluding gluten from his diet improved his focus and concentration, maintained his energy levels and enabled him to regain control of his emotions.

In 2011 Djokavic finally achieved his dream of winning Wimbledon and became the number one tennis player in the world. He won 43 matches in a row, 50 out of 51 tournaments over a 12 month period. In 2011, he won 10 titles, three grand slams and 43 consecutive matches. He later was named by Time Magazine as one of the top 100 most influential people in the world. Djokovic later won the ESPN Best Male Tennis player award and was the flag bearer for Serbia in the 2012 Olympics. In that same year he received the Arthur Ashe Humanitarian of the Year.

Djokovic reports in his book that he did not change anything in his training, practice and daily routine other than exclude gluten from his diet. Djokovic makes it crystal clear that none of the above accomplishments would have occurred if he continued to consume gluten.

Djokovic only learned to avoid gluten as a result of allowing Dr. Cetojevic to use a form of Applied Kinesiology. This same method contributed to the field of energy psychology and to the creation of PPO. It cannot be emphasized enough that you do not have to have an extreme negative reaction to a substance like Novak Djokovic had, but that a hypersensitivity can weaken you, hurt your tennis game and block the benefits you can derive from PPO.

CHAPTER 10

THE NEED TO TAKE LESSONS FROM A TEACHING PRO

The aspect of tennis that PPO can impact the greatest is the psychological, or, now it is commonly referred to, the "mental" side. The vast majority of tennis instruction and lessons are on the physical fundamentals and technical aspects. There are very few people who can have great improvement in how they play on the tennis courts without taking lessons. There are many instructors who give excellent information and who are patient and caring about your improvement. I have experienced and observed this over and over in all the years I have been involved with tennis. The odds are extremely low that you can transform your game into consistently good shot-making or serving simply by relying on a book or video. The effects of PPO are usually limited if there are fundamental flaws in your strokes and you do not take lessons.

I will be using the word "stroke" to refer to any stroke or serve that you are trying to transform. Transforming a stroke means that you have developed the ability to hit it in an entirely different and more effective way than what you had been doing that produced less than acceptable results. This also applies to when you hit the original stoke with some effectiveness, but clearly have room to improve if you can hit in a different, better way. Complete transformation occurs when you can hit the stroke competently in competitive matches. Refining a stroke is making some change to improve on hitting what is essentially an adequate stroke. When you go from getting fair results because you rely on a flat or slice forehand, but now can play better because you added an effective topspin forehand, you have transformed the stroke. Being able to get even more of a slice or kick in a serve because you have made some change on how you hit it is an example of a refinement.

Transforming your stroke or serve is difficult because of a phenomenon known as muscle memory, the physical state of being that is difficult to change. It develops because you physically have done a certain motion or action repeatedly throughout your life, or, in this case, since you started playing tennis. When a movement is repeated over time, a long-term muscle memory is created for that task, eventually allowing it to be performed without conscious effort. It essentially becomes effortless.

We experience muscle memory all the time. Examples in everyday life include riding a bicycle, typing on a keyboard or putting in a password when logging in. Our mind and body carry out these actions with little thought. Isn't it amazing that you can go years without riding a bicycle and very quickly resume riding again? Almost everyone takes this for granted and does not wonder why this is possible. Reconstructing a stroke or serve is more difficult when you have relied on your original stroke for a long time and over the many times you have played. To improve a stroke that you have repeatedly done is an attempt to alter the extremely powerful force of muscle memory. It is not your intention to prevent this change from happening, or that you do not understand the goal you want to achieve. It is simply a difficult mind-body transformation.

However, even for long-time players, it is possible to make fundamental changes in your stroke with the assistance of PPO.

A child or adult first learning the game should get lessons. By learning right from the start how to hit the ball correctly, you not only get results when you begin to play tennis, but you also are preventing any negative muscle memory developing and obstructing progress.

Repeated experience for myself and clients revealed that Psychological Reversals frequently need to be treated to transform a stroke that you have been hitting a certain way for a long time. This only makes sense. Trying to get your body to do something so entirely different than what is deeply embedded would be a process of reversing what exists because of muscle memory. As a result of muscle memory, Psychological Reversals must be treated and repeatedly eliminated. In addition to changing a stroke through repeated instruction and lessons, overtaking muscle memory also requires determination, repeated practice and patience. When you are tense, muscle memory increases the likelihood that you will slip back to the original stroke. A difficult part of changing the stroke is having the psychological ability and willingness to tolerate a potential temporary deterioration of your game. Using PPO can help you through this process.

You can benefit from applying PPO at any time during the process of trying to improve your stroke or serve. There are always emotions that could limit your progress. The most frequent are frustration, anger, impatience and getting discouraged. Nervousness and tension usually occur when you are trying to use the new stroke in very competitive or important matches. This is especially true if you do not hit it successfully the first few times. Changing a stroke or serve is the time when Distress and Belief Ratings can be given in different rounds of PPO.

It is important to share with your instructors that you are applying PPO. Don't be surprised if they are unaware of this method or do not believe it will help. It is not necessary for your coach to believe PPO can help. You both can notice over time whether there has been a difference, compared to earlier times you took lessons. The pace and success of change can vary depending on how different it is and the length of time you have been hitting the ball with that old stroke. However, when you make this change more easily it is worthwhile to point it out to your instructor. Suggest the instructor look at the descriptions that applies to tennis instructors at: **PerformAtPeak.com/coaches**

An additional benefit is that you will find yourself more attuned to which teaching pros are most helpful. Communication usually improves. You can also be less timid about asking questions or disagreeing with your instructors. There can be a realization that you need to work with just one coach. There are times when making the change is not reasonable. You may have been hitting the original stroke for decades and do not intensely care enough if the new stroke will develop. Even then PPO can be helpful recognizing and accepting that this is the case.

PPO Procedure for Players to Benefit from Lessons

Unless you are an exceptional athlete, transforming a stroke requires applying PPO and taking lessons. One set of PPO sessions and tennis lessons are usually not enough. Combining both a few times is usually required especially if you have not succeeded in transforming the stroke from past lessons. Incorporating PPO will make the transition be quicker.

I recommend that you write your answers on the pages below or on one of the copies of Appendix 1 or 2. Earlier chapters had the picture location of acupressure points that you tap. In addition, the sequence of acupressure points you tap for different emotions has been specified. That information does not appear here. If you need it, simply go back to chapter 7. Reconstructing a stroke is difficult. It almost always requires taking lessons, doing the PPO procedure, practicing and playing important or competitive matches. After deciding what stroke you want to transform, the next decision is about using the Past or the Future Perspective Protocols. Most players want to get immediate results. In that case, the Future Perspective Protocol is used. There is no problem with this choice except if you have tried to learn these new strokes for a long time but were frustrated or upset that you were unable to do so even though you repeatedly took lessons. The fact that you had upsetting experiences means that emotional factors are likely to interfere with your benefiting from PPO, and the obstructive effects of those experiences should first be eliminated. If that is the case, you would start using PPO with the Past Perspective Protocol in Appendix 2 or on page 145.

Applying the Future Perspective Protocol
for Transforming a Stroke

If you are applying the Future Perspective Protocol, it means you will be thinking of taking a lesson and then eventually being able to hit the new stroke with relative consistency in important matches. It is the end result that counts. You don't want to be just hitting the new stroke during the lesson or when practicing. The focus in the future perspective is not on the lesson itself but on picturing yourself hitting your newly constructed stroke.

Think about and picture yourself playing well. Hitting the new stroke is coming easily, almost to the point of being effortless. The match gets closer. All of a sudden you start mishitting the shot a number of times. You begin to feel yourself tense up. Maybe you start wondering if you should go back to the old way that you hit the ball. Now you are switching back and forth and feel like you've lost control of what you're supposed to do. You are losing points. To make matters worse, you are hitting almost all of your strokes poorly. You can picture this experience as a photograph, or see it occurring over time as you would with a video.

Write the emotion or body sensations you are having right now at this moment.

_____

_____

_____

_____

Rate the intensity from 0 - 10.

Distress Rating =_____

You can write Distress or Belief Ratings on the forms below. If you are not feeling any negative emotions or body sensations, answer this question:

"Even though I will take lessons, I will not be able to consistently hit the new stroke in important matches."

Zero indicates that you believe that you will be able to hit the new stroke in important matches. Ten indicates that the above statement is absolutely true.

Belief Rating = _____

The sequence of acupressure Points for steps 2 and 4 will be the Comprehensive Acupressure Tapping Sequence (CATS). This is necessary because no negative emotions could be identified.

First Round

1) Eliminate the Psychological Reversals:

Tap on the karate spot (Acupressure Point 1) and say three times:

"I deeply and profoundly accept myself with all my problems and limitations."

Pause a few seconds. Tap on the karate spot (Acupressure Point 1) and say three times:

"Even though I have this problem, I deeply accept myself."

Tap under your nose (Acupressure Point 2) and say three times:

"I deeply accept myself even if I never get completely over this problem."

Distress Rating = _____   Belief Rating = _____

(Recall that your Distress Rating may not go down from treating the reversals. This procedure removes the blocks that impede progress.)

2) Apply CATS.

3-4-5-6-7-5-8-9-2-11-5-10-5

How intense are you experiencing the negative emotion at this moment? Give a rating from 0-10.

   Distress Rating = _____   Belief Rating = _____

3) Brain Balance Procedure:

While you continuously tap on the 10th Acupressure Point, you are to simultaneously:

   a) Close your eyes.
   b) Open your eyes and look straight ahead.
   c) Move your eyes to 5:00 on a clock by looking down to your right.
   d) Move your eyes to 7:00 on a clock, by looking down to your left.
   e) Circle your eyes clockwise for two revolutions.
   f) Circle your eyes counterclockwise for 2 revolutions.
   g) Hum high and low notes without words.
   h) Count to 5 out loud.
   i) Hum high and low notes.

How intense are you experiencing the negative emotion or body sensation at this moment? Give a rating from 0-10.

   Distress Rating = _____   Belief Rating = _____

4) Apply CATS.

How intense are you experiencing the negative emotion or body sensations at this moment? Give rating from 0-10. If you are not feeling any distress, give a Belief Rating

  Distress Rating = _____   Belief Rating = _____

If your Distress or Belief Rating is 2 or less, do the Eye Roll Procedure. You have now completed one round of PPO. Even if your Distress or Belief Rating is zero, you still are to do three rounds.

You will now follow the same steps as you did in the first round.

Second Round

  Distress Rating = _____   Belief Rating = _____

Eliminate the Specific Psychological Reversal by Tapping on the karate spot (Acupressure Point 1) and say three times:

"Even though I have this problem, I deeply accept myself."

  Distress Rating =_____   Belief Rating = _____

2) Apply CATS.

  Distress Rating = _____   Belief Rating = _____

3) Do Brain Balance Procedure.

  Distress Rating = _____   Belief Rating = _____

4) Apply CATS.

  Distress Rating = _____   Belief Rating = _____

If the Distress or Belief Rating is a 1 or 2, apply the Eye Roll Procedure.

Distress Rating = _____   Belief Rating = _____

Even if your Distress or Belief Rating is zero, you still are to do the third round.

Third Round

Distress Rating = _____   Belief Rating = _____

Eliminate the Specific Psychological Reversal by Tapping on the karate spot (Acupressure Point 1) and say three times:

"Even though I have this problem, I deeply accept myself."

Distress Rating = _____   Belief Rating = _____

2) Apply CATS.

3) Do Brain Balance Procedure.

Distress Rating = _____   Belief Rating = _____

4) Apply CATS.

Distress Rating = _____   Belief Rating = _____

If the Distress or Belief Rating is a 1 or 2, apply the Eye Roll Procedure.

Distress Rating = _____   Belief Rating = _____

Important Assessment: I would recommend taking a lesson in the near future. You can take a lesson at any time, but will most likely benefit from your lessons when you are in a relaxed state and more confident.

Is your Distress Rating 2 or above? If so, apply the Past Perspective Protocol

Applying the Past Perspective Protocol for Transforming a Stroke

Think about this stroke or serve that you want to change. Recall the times when you were hitting the new stroke poorly even though you had taken lessons. Give yourself time to reflect on that. Try to remember that experience clearly. Maybe you were confident that you were going to play great after taking a lesson, but then went out and played terrible. Maybe others saw you play poorly at that time and lost to an inferior player. Remember those moments so clearly that it almost seems like yesterday when it occurred. Keep doing so to activate a negative emotion or body sensation. When thinking about this upsetting experience, you can picture it as a photograph or see it occurring over time as you would with a video.

Write about that experience:

_____

_____

_____

_____

Write the emotion or body sensations you are having right now at this moment. You are not to write down what you were feeling during that experience. What counts is the current feelings you are now experiencing.

_____

_____

_____

Since you are going back to a past experience, only Distress Ratings are to be given.

How intense are you experiencing the negative emotion at this moment? Give a rating from 0-10.

Distress Rating = _____

(Since you are bringing up an upsetting memory, there is no need for belief ratings when you apply the Past Perspective Protocol.)

1) Eliminate the Psychological Reversals:

Tap on the karate spot (Acupressure Point 1) and say three times:

"I deeply and profoundly accept myself with all my problems and limitations."

Pause a few seconds. Tap on the karate spot (Acupressure Point 1) and say three times:

"Even though I have this problem, I deeply accept myself."

Tap under your nose (Acupressure Point 2) and say three times:

"I deeply accept myself even if I never get completely over this problem."

Distress Rating = _____

(Recall that your Distress Rating may not go down from treating the reversals. This procedure removes the blocks that impede progress.)

2) Apply CATS.

How intense are you experiencing the negative emotion at this moment? Give a rating from 0-100.

Distress Rating = _____

3) Brain Balance Procedure:

While you continuously tap on the 10th Acupressure Point, you are to simultaneously:

a) Close your eyes.
b) Open your eyes and look straight ahead.
c) Move your eyes to 5:00 on a clock by looking down to your right.
d) Move your eyes to 7:00 on a clock, by looking down to your left.
e) Circle your eyes clockwise for two revolutions.
f) Circle your eyes counterclockwise for two revolutions.
g) Hum high and low notes without words.
h) Count to 5 out loud.
i) Hum high and low notes.

How intense are you experiencing the negative emotion or body sensation at this moment? Give a rating from 0-100.

Distress Rating = _____

4) Apply CATS.

How intense are you experiencing the negative emotion or body sensations at this moment? Give rating from 0-100.

Distress Rating = _____

If your Distress Rating is 2 or less, do the Eye Roll Procedure. You have now completed one round of PPO for this negative emotion or body sensation. Even if your Distress Rating is zero, you still are to do three rounds.

You will now follow the same steps as you did in the first round.

Second Round

Distress Rating = _____

Eliminate the Specific Psychological Reversal by Tapping on the karate spot (Acupressure Point 1) and say three times:

"Even though I have this problem, I deeply accept myself."

Distress Rating = _____

2) Apply CATS.

Distress Rating = _____

3) Do Brain Balance Procedure.

Distress Rating = _____

2) Apply CATS.

Distress Rating = _____

If the Distress Rating is a 1 or 2, apply the Eye Roll Procedure.

Distress Rating = _____

Even if your Distress Rating is zero, you still are to do the third round.

Third Round

Distress Rating = _____

Emotion or body sensations = _____

SQ = _____

Eliminate the Specific Psychological Reversal by Tapping on the karate spot (Acupressure Point 1) and say three times:

"Even though I have this problem, I deeply accept myself."

Distress Rating = _____

Distress Rating = _____

2) Do SQ.

3) Do Brain Balance Procedure.

Distress Rating = _____

4) Repeat SQ.

Distress Rating = _____

If the Distress Rating is a 1 or 2, apply the Eye Roll Procedure.

Distress Rating = _____

No matter what your Distress Rating is, you now apply PPO using the Future Perspective Protocol. Write your answers on the copy you made of Appendix 1.

Keep in mind that lessons and your application of PPO throughout this process is very important. Keep taking lessons, apply PPO, practice, be patient and play matches that are important. You will eventually transform the stroke.

When Trying to Transform a Stroke, the Best Times to Apply PPO are:

Right after a match in which you play poorly.

Right after a match where you were tense or tentative about using the new stroke or serve.

When you are mad or frustrated at yourself or your tennis instructor.

Being upset that a lesson or practice session did not go well.

When you are losing confidence that you will be able to consistently hit the new stroke or serve.

It is not unusual to resort back to hitting the old undesired stroke after thinking you have mastered the transformed stroke that you desired. It is particularly frustrating when you think you have mastered the stroke, only to lose it. Muscle memory tends to make this a back and forth process.

You probably will find other times when it is best to use PPO. Trust your intuition. Any time you're feeling bad in any type of way is an opportunity to have PPO help you.

Lessons Transform a Backhand

Denise is a 37-year-old woman who repeatedly took lessons to learn how to hit a topspin backhand. In all her playing years she hit a slice backhand any time she could. Muscle memory was formed and would make the conversion to a topspin backhand difficult. The slice was relatively effective when playing singles, but this was not the case in doubles. Both opponents knew she relied on the slice. It was only a matter of time that this softer shot would get up too high and make it easy for opponents to come to the net and hit winners.

Denise had taken almost all her lessons with the same instructor but was unable to consistently hit the desired stroke in competitive matches. In fact, there was a deterioration in the accuracy and speed of her slice backhand. This is not an unusual occurrence and is an example of how muscle memory makes it difficult to make the transition to a new stroke. When we discussed this problem in our first PPO session over the Internet she gave a

Belief Rating of 7. Once we started the PPO process she reported feeling frustrated. This was quickly eliminated by using the Past Perspective Protocol. This led us to shift to the Future Perspective Protocol, where she tried to imagine being able to master the ability to hit both backhands. I asked about her thoughts that she would be able to consistently hit a topspin and slice backhand in a match. Denise then felt apprehensive but this was eliminated after three rounds of PPO.

After two lessons from the same instructor and continued practice her backhand improved, but not when playing matches. Subsequent lessons did not ameliorate this pattern of results. Denise experienced annoyance with herself when discussing this problem in our next PPO session. After this feeling stayed at 2 even with repeated rounds, she gave a Belief rating of 6 when she thought about her ability to make this transition. Treatment of this belief led to feelings of doubt that were treated and eliminated as the session progressed.

After only taking one more lesson she started playing better in competitive matches. However, she noticed that her body would stiffen. Denise memorized how to apply PPO without me, and these body sensations decreased. Sure enough, she was able to hit slice and topspin backhands more frequently with less unforced errors. Although this ability fluctuated, this transformation finally occurred. Her subsequent improvement to also hit winners at the net with her backhand is an example of how an additional improvement occurs as a result of the generalization of the effects of PPO.

CHAPTER 11

ANCIENT HEALING AND PEAK PERFORMANCE OPTIMIZATION

There are no comprehensive explanations of how an athlete suddenly is playing so great that we would think he or she is playing in a zone. Writers, commentators, and athletes conclude that a player is in a zone only during or after such displays of excellence. Most athletes who have such experiences cannot describe in detail how this came to be for that particular match or game. If they could, it would be duplicated more frequently. No one has provided an explanatory model of what psychophysiological and biological systems would correspond with an athlete playing in a zone or at their peak.

Such an explanatory model exists, but has never been connected to peak performance before. Acupuncture has existed for more than 4,000 years and has been the basis for healthcare for centuries. Acupuncture and acupressure stimulate the physiological and energy systems that became the basis of Traditional Chinese Medicine. Although much more is written about acupuncture, researchers demonstrated that under certain circumstances, tapping can have powerful and therapeutic effects.

This chapter is for those who want to better understand how working with the acupressure system can lead one to function at heightened levels of performance. It is only recently that acupressure stimulation has been linked to optimal performance in sports and is the basis for Peak Performance Optimization (PPO). This chapter is not about advocating and recommending acupuncture treatment for a tennis player. The purpose of this chapter is to help you understand how the Chinese theory and practice of acupressure provide a basis to understand peak performance.

The Chinese discovered more than four centuries ago a system in which vital energies flow through the body. Through astute observation and by trial and error over centuries, acupuncturists discovered that certain parts of the body could heal numerous symptoms and diseases. This led to the development of the Traditional Chinese Medicine. The Chinese referred to this energy as Qi (pronounced as "Cheee"). Energy in this explanatory model is not thought of as being fatigued or invigorated, but as a life force within and throughout the body.

Energy (Qi) Travels in a Specific Manner: The forces of energy flow through body channels. These are called meridian pathways that have starting and ending points. Energy is ideally flowing in one direction to promote health and optimal benefits.

These meridians are thought of as an energy highway where energy permeates the entire body and mind and affects all other physiological and neurological systems. There are 12 meridians. There are also two vessels that essentially function as meridians. The Chinese found that there are spots on the body that are very sensitive to biomechanical stimulation impulses along these 14 pathways.

There are a total of 365 acupressure points on the body. These specific points on the body are where acupuncturists insert needles. Figure 1 shows the location of some acupressure points. Note that these points are on lines, which are the pathways of how they are interconnected.

Ideally there is a flow of Qi such that energy forces are in a harmonious balance between yin and yang. Many of the health problems in modern society come from living in a society that is very different than that which existed when the human species first evolved. There were not any 8-10-hour work days, processed food, water pollution and exposure to all types of man-made chemicals. Any alterations of this ideal state make one vulnerable to illness and dysfunction.

Figure 1 Some of the 365 Acupressure Points

You can liken this energy meridian system to a complex railroad system where energy travels along certain tracks in one expansive system. Each train stop is similar to an acupressure point in that they both have a heightened state of activity in such locations. Research has determined that these spots on the body exhibit additional physical characteristics such as the conduction of infrared radiation, light and microwaves, enhanced ultrasound attenuation and less electromagnetic resistance. Like the flow of people at a train stop, meridians are where more energetic activity occurs within the body. The energy meridian system is like a chain of many railroad tracks traveling at one time. The energy of meridians is constantly flowing. When each train travels in the correct direction and speed, the railroad system functions efficiently. Trains that do not follow the correct direction can result in disastrous consequences. Trains that travel too slowly and do not arrive at their scheduled times can cause excessive congestion throughout the system for a period of time. This also can occur in the body's 14 meridians, where life energy can be impeded, poorly coordinated, or blocked, causing an energetic imbalance.

Locating meridians in the body: Getting images of energy meridians had been elusive because of the lack of advanced instruments, causing scientists and physicians to doubt they even existed. Energy meridians do not directly correspond with structures of the nervous, lymphatic or circulatory system but, in fact, affect these systems. The inability to get a visual image of a phenomenon does not mean that phenomenon does not exist. Broken bones existed before we had x-rays to provide a picture of what they looked like. The structure and function of the nervous system always existed, but became more understandable after CT scans, MRIs and EMG tests were developed. Fortunately, developments in medical devices have enabled demonstration of the acupressure pathways. A study in the "Proceedings of the National Academy of Science" used functional magnetic resonance imaging (fMRI) to demonstrate that stimulating certain acupressure point activated a specific point in the brain. It did not follow any of the other traditional anatomical structures. Further evidence of the existence of these acupressure points was provided by a special camera that registers bio photons in a specific range. Stimulation of an acupressure point produced bio photons and light that is identical to the pathways the Chinese acupuncturists mapped out two thousand years ago. The pathways of energy meridians described in acupuncture correspond to the pathways of intramuscular and intramuscular connective tissue. Semi-connective tissue enables acupuncture to rapidly send electromagnetic signals to specific areas in the body and mind.

Research in Acupuncture and Acupressure

One requirement that any explanatory model would have to meet before it can be considered to explain peak performance in athletes would be research that proves that interventions into the acupressure system helps human functioning. In their review of research of the highest quality of scientific standards, the World Health Organization has found that acupuncture has been proven to significantly help 24 diseases and symptoms.

Conditions in which acupuncture treatment is most relevant to athletics are:

Tennis elbow
Facial pain, including craniomandibular disorders
Headache
Knee pain
Low back pain
Neck pain
Pain in dentistry (including dental pain and temporomandibular dysfunction such as TMJ)
Periarthritis of shoulder
Postoperative pain
Rheumatoid arthritis
Sciatica
Sprain

When compared to acupuncture, there are many more research studies demonstrating the efficacy of acupressure on human behavior, emotional problems, and factors that lead to less than optimal functioning.

A review of 33 research studies on the effectiveness of acupressure stimulation found that that these techniques result in a reduction of such conditions as test-taking anxiety, emotional distress, claustrophobia, phobias, public-speaking and food cravings. Almost all studies did not base conclusions solely on self-report, but were also validated on psychological tests. These methods were effective even when administered by different types of providers, some of which were not licensed mental health workers or professionals. These providers can only be effective because acupressure stimulation is such a positive and powerful method.

Most importantly, there are a number of research studies that demonstrate that acupressure stimulation reduces emotional problems. Such negative emotions as sustained anger, anxiety, apprehension, continuously occur after traumatic events. Traumatic experiences before adulthood, especially at younger ages, can lead to pathological symptoms and disorders. Research on acupressure stimulation has continuously found that acupressure methods are extremely effective.

Acupressure is the Basis for Peak Performance Optimization

Fortunately, it was discovered that there are alternative methods to stimulate the acupuncture energy meridian system. In contrast to acupuncture, acupressure does not involve using needles to pierce the skin. There are many acupressure methods that are simpler, gentler, and safer than acupuncture. Most forms of acupressure use the fingers to stimulate acupressure points, which activate the body's natural self-healing capabilities. Shiatsu, Reiki, and Reflexology are some of the better known acupressure treatment modalities. Professionals provide acupressure services to facilitate mental alertness and clarity, concentration, improved sleep, restoration of range of motion after muscular-skeletal injuries and for some degree of pain relief. The fact that PPO only requires tapping the two fingertips makes it extremely easy to apply.

Most coaching methods about the mental aspects of peak performance specify a number of steps and strategies. Such programs have a basic structure and sequence. They require an athlete to repeatedly observe and think about specific instructions and then to repeatedly practice to obtain and sustain peak performance. Under these systems, there is a forcefulness and determination of will that enables a certain pace of improvement. Even when doing so, few athletes will report that they perform at their potential, especially for any extended time period. Excessive force generally inhibits and impedes being in a flow in the actual match, especially when under pressure. Incorporating acupressure stimulation in any coaching method more easily enables peak performance. The PPO method transforms the energy in the in the meridian system to travel in the correct energetic imbalance does not preclude obtaining heightened states of consciousness and performance. Only then can the body and mind function synergistically. Energy travels easily and effortlessly, just like the flow an athlete experiences when performing at their peak.

CHAPTER 12

THE NEUROLOGICAL BASIS FOR PEAK PERFORMANCE OPTIMIZATION

Any changes in behavior and athletic performance obviously has to involve the brain. It is estimated that there are 10 billion to 100 billion cells in the brain, known as neurons and that there are 100 billion wires connecting all neurons. Although this is an incredible to imagine numerous scientific writings continue to make such estimations. A neuron is an electrically excitable cell that processes and transmits information through electrical and chemical signals. Each neuron connects to numerous other neurons through wire-like structures known as axons and dendrites. A single firing neuron may stimulate thousands of others in a single moment. All mental and physical functioning is based independently on the development, maintenance, and modification of the neuron networks.

Brain Centers for Thought and Emotions

The outer layer of the brain is the cerebral cortex, the most highly developed part, responsible for thinking, perceiving, producing and understanding language. It is the most recent structure in the history of brain evolution. It resides over and around most of the structures of the brain and encompasses about two-thirds of the mass. The cerebral cortex consists of up to six horizontal layers, each with a different composition in terms of neurons and connectivity. The cerebral cortex is divided into right and left hemispheres. Within each there are four large regions or lobes: the frontal, occipital, temporal, and parietal. Any advice that is given is processed in the cerebral cortex.

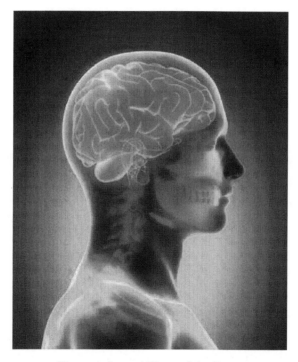

Figure 1: Lateral View of the Brain

The Emotional Brain: The primary region of the brain for emotions is the limbic system, referred to as the emotional region of the brain. The limbic system is involved in such emotions as anxiety, anger, apprehension, shame, stubbornness, disgust, resignation and impatience, guilt and embarrassment. The limbic system is located in the midbrain which is centrally located. There are millions of wires, known as axons and dendrites, connecting it to the upper and lower regions of the brain. It is the set of structures that forms the inner border of the cortex. It is below parts of the brain responsible for thinking, decision making, problem solving and planning, memory, hearing and language. It is also mostly above the regions of the brain that regulate the most basic of human functioning and survival, such as movement, coordination, breathing and the continued beating of the heart.

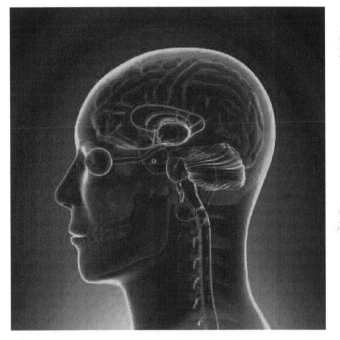

Figure 2: The middle area is the location of the
limbic system and the midbrain

There are a number of important implications of the central location of this emotional region. Many neurological circuits integrate the most complex thinking with the most basic structures in the brain and facilitate the connections among the mind, body and athletic performance. It is not only the limbic system and midbrain's central location that causes it to have such powerful effects on the emotions we experience. The amount of wires or projections originating from the central region of the brain to the cerebral brain are substantially greater than the amount of wires originating from the cerebral cortex that go to the limbic system. As a result, it is not difficult for emotions to interfere with thinking during athletic performance.

Instructions and Rates of Improvement in Tennis: All forms of instruction and teaching in tennis are processed in the cerebral cortex. This is true if a teaching pro is talking to you, demonstrating a stroke or verbalizing what you need to correct. This is also true when you visualize yourself playing, watching an instructional video, and thinking about past matches.

There are many great instructors, organized clinics, schools, and mental and physical training that are provided by numerous instructors, clubs, and academies around the world. The coaching instruction typically given occurs through words which go to the left hemisphere of the cerebral cortex. If you are told to picture or have an image of how to do the desired action, you are then stimulating the right hemisphere of the outer layer of your brain. Most coaching and even psychotherapy is based on interventions that try to change the way you think so that eventually it will change how you feel, behave, and perform. This means that the information only goes to the integrative area of the brain only after it is processed in the cerebral cortex. However, the vast majority of neural connections that first go into the cerebral cortex are from one area of the cortex to another. There are substantially less neural connections that go from the cerebral cortex directly to the midbrain. This means that only a fraction of the information and instruction that is given by words affects the emotional and integrative regions of the brain. No matter how great tennis instruction is the means of transmitting information is going through a slower pathway that ultimately limits how much your abilities can increase.

The Unconscious Region of the Brain

The idea that there is an unconscious region of the brain that has a powerful impact on emotions and behavioral disorders originated with the psychiatrist Sigmund Freud, who taught that there are forces people are not conscious of yet exert a powerful effect on overall psychological functioning and behavior. Freud's theories became a paradigm for the treatment of mental health disorders and their treatment for decades. According to Freud, the unconscious mind is a reservoir and the origination of impulses, feelings, thoughts, wishes and memories that are outside of conscious awareness. Much of adult personality and problems originate from early childhood experiences. Freud viewed the unconscious region of the brain as larger as and more powerful than the conscious. An image of this was provided in chapter 1. Athletes are eventually taught to react, and not overthink.

The development of the limbic system and midbrain precedes that of the cerebral cortex. This is consistent with the finding that there are more wires projecting into the cortex compared to wires originating from the cerebral cortex to the limbic system. Such circuits and networks of neurons are originating from the lower regions of the brain.

Although many of Freud's theories has been proven wrong or modified the concept of an unconscious region of the brain has essentially become indisputable. This is not to say that his treatment methods were effective in short periods of time or that his theories has not been disputed for decades. However research has revealed that automatically, and clearly outside of conscious awareness, individuals register and acquire more information than what they can experience through their conscious thoughts. For example, a series of research studies has demonstrated that individuals register information about the frequency of events automatically. This would be recognition not in conscious awareness. Perceivers do this unintentionally or automatically regardless of the instructions they receive and of the information processing goals they have.

Here is another way for understanding this theory that the unconscious can have long standing obstructive problems. Have you noticed the following?

You give good advice to someone and they agree with it, but are unable to change their behavior. A workaholic is told by friends that they are working too hard, are looking tired and ragged, and that they "are working themselves to death." The person knows this to be true. Their physician has warned them to work less and exercise more or else they will need to be on blood pressure and cholesterol medicine, and even have a second heart attack. The patient leaves the doctor's office determined to work less and exercise more. However, this eventually does not occur. His wife and children reminds him that he was going to make this change. The continuous work and lack of exercise reflects the belief of him verbalizing "I know that I have to change things, but right now I am busy with very important work."

Pay attention to how much this occurs with others. It takes the form of:

"I agree, but _____" or something to the effect of "Yes, that is true but_____." These are "yes, but" statements.

"It is easy to say, but hard to do." Things may change temporarily, but the person returns back to their old unsatisfying or unhealthy ways. They know that it is not right, but are unable to make or maintain the change

Saying "yes" is recognition that the advice is correct. The "but" reflects the brain's inability to completely incorporate and act on the sensible advice. The information is coming through and being processed in the cerebral cortex, but existing neural connections emanating from the unconscious preclude making the change. This is why "You can't teach an old dog new tricks.

This is also applicable to you. Think about how many times you have been given good advice that you agree with and yet you have not changed your behavior or performance. It could simply be something you know to be true and yet not follow.

An example of this is unhealthy eating patterns that keep many people obese. They may be enrolled in an expensive diet program that provides a number of sensible guidelines. Once again instructions are given to cut down on the size of portions, stop eating deserts so much, begin to exercise regularly, and do not eat late at night. Not only do all of them agree with such advice, but have heard this over and over from many people. They can be dieting properly all day and at night have ice cream, blowing the entire effort for the day, no less exacerbating the problem. Before you know it, they are barely exercising and sneaking sweets. The obese person runs into people who do not understand that the commitment to losing weight is actually sincere. At such times their statements are coming from the conscious rational mind. One may very much want to lose weight, but forces unknown prevent preclude change. This is the power of the unconscious mind.

I am sure you know this to be true of others and for yourself in some form or manner. No matter how motivated and determined, you eventually slip back to your old and self-defeating patterns. Although the above examples may not describe you, just think of some of the things that you do, that underneath it all, you know are not good for you, self-limiting, or cause unnecessary suffering for you and others. How many times have you done something that you know is wrong or had bad results before, but make the mistake of doing it one more time again, maybe two, three.........more times. The brain is structured and organized such that change and the ability to act on it is difficult.

This is also true in tennis. You can be given cogent advice on how to hit a stroke. You have heard it before from different teaching pros and even observed it watching friends or pros on television. You keep trying to change and improve, but ultimately are unable to do so. The difficulty in being able to continuously maintain the improved stroke you are being taught is because the instruction is first coming into the outer layer of the brain and has a limited effect on the emotional and integrative regions of the brain that ultimately prevent or greatly limit improvement.

He Just Could Not Resist Trying to Hit Winners: This "yes, but" problem existed with one of my clients. Joe had a relatively simple problem and was aware of it. He would try to hit winners too often, whether it was from the baseline or when coming in to hit a volley. He was in great shape and could run down balls better than his friends. He didn't have to try to hit so many winners because he had the capacity to be consistent by just keeping the ball in and hitting it past the service line. Joe was aware that he was hitting the ball out too often when trying to hit winners, but continued to play this way. He loved the feeling of hitting a great shot and placing the ball right near or on the lines. Unfortunately, this would lead him to increasingly try to play aggressively, even though he knew that this typically led him to hit unforced errors, leading him to lose matches he really could and should have won. An additional part of this problem was when he would try to hit winners in the beginning of the match and continue to do so even when the ball would go out. He would stubbornly continue to try to find his shot even though this was not working, believing it was just a matter of time before playing this way would be successful. This obviously led to him falling behind too frequently. He knew he had this problem, but was unable to break this pattern. He was not a stupid man, but a successful businessman. It is just that when it came to tennis, his neural circuitry was wired such that he could not break this self-defeating pattern.

Although the vast amount of athletes and coaches might disagree, the rate of improvement from conventional instruction methods is ultimately slow in tennis or any sport. Unfortunately they were never taught about such processes and principles of neurology and the power of acupressure. The nature and organization of the brain processes limits the amount of improvement from any instruction that is directed to the conscious mind and does not have the ability to also stimulate and activate unconscious processes. This is true whether the instruction is coming from lessons, clinics, or videos. Improvement from conventional type lessons requires much teaching, practice and repetition. As described, obstacles to improving usually involve the neural circuitry and projections from the unconscious mind that make it difficult to change and rapidly get better at tennis Even though instructors are tremendously talented, almost all have not learned or even been exposed to methods that more directly stimulate the most influential neuron networks.

The main point for tennis players and coaches is that they will only get substantially better in their abilities when methods are utilized that have a global and holistic effect on neurological functioning. The unconscious has a powerful effect on emotional reactions, pace of learning, impeding progress, and the enjoyment from playing this and any other sport. Instructors would be more effective if they could combine the teaching of technical skills and strategy along with such procedures as Peak Performance Optimization (PPO). The combination of conventional coaching methods with acupressure stimulation produces more effective results. PPO just makes it easier for one to improve their game from any good tennis instructor. The coach can enjoy the more rapid progress their clients obtain.

Sometimes an athlete purposely stays away from teammates to avoid thinking about what they are in the midst of achieving, helping them to sustain their great level of athletic performance. Continuous thinking will shift neurological activity away from the unconscious.

The baseball teammates of a pitcher will not sit near him when he is pitching a perfect game, where the other team does not have any hits or even gotten on base. The teammates of a basketball player who is playing great will leave him alone or the player himself will not talk to his teammates. This happened in a basketball game where Kobe Bryant scored the second most points in the history of pro basketball. Bryant stayed away from the team's huddle with the coach during the timeouts. Involving him in discussion could break the spell and take him out of the zone he was in.

Isn't it interesting that when an athlete is playing great that players, announcers and fans verbalize such phrases as?

"He is unconscious."

"He is playing out of his mind."

"He is in the zone."

Neuroplasticity

By this point you might think that no significant change can occur for some players due to the unconscious dynamic and the way that the brain is wired. Before the advent of neurological imaging equipment, the brain was thought of as a physiologically static organ. Neurologists and researchers believed that changes in the brain could only take place during infancy and childhood, that the brain's physical structure was permanent and unable to significantly change in its neural pathways. Such an opinion would clearly be consistent with what is being described about neuron networks that originate from or are connected to the unconscious. It would be discouraging if change was not possible.

However, this is not the case. A number of studies over recent years have led scientists to conclude that neurological circuitry can change at the sub-cortical levels, and they have defined this area of science as neuroplasticity. It refers to changes in neural pathways and synapses. A number of studies have now demonstrated that substantial changes occur in the lowest neocortical processing areas, and that these changes can profoundly alter the pattern of neuronal activation. Modern research has demonstrated that the brain continues to create neural pathways. There can be change in both the brain's physical structure (anatomy) and functional organization (physiology).

Acupressure stimulation within traditional coaching methods is a very effective method to alter brain functioning at the sub-cortical level. A number of studies have shown that acupressure methods change the nature of brain wave activity. This has been associated with decreases of distress, anxiety, and tension. PPO employs these methods, with the result that superior athletic performance occurs.

CHAPTER 13

BE GREAT IN ANY SPORT AND IN LIFE

S ignificant and quick improvement in sports from Peak Performance Optimization (PPO) is not limited to tennis. PPO is a method that can be applied to any sport where emotional reactions and thought patterns limit the level of performance in any one competition or over a period of time. This method has been very successful in elevating performance and increasing enjoyment of golf, baseball, basketball, gymnastics or martial arts, among others.

Significant improvement occurs quickly because PPO simultaneously improves thought patterns, emotional reactions, body sensations and behaviors while playing the sport. The major intervention of this acupressure method quickly affects the limbic system in the brain, where there are an enormous amount of neural connections that cause many physiological and psychological responses.

There are a number of treatment and coaching systems that have been developed where acupressure stimulation is a major component. Most of these interventions are based on the discoveries

Dr. Roger Callahan developed in his clinical practice. Dr. Callahan was incredibly intelligent, curious, creative and insightful and this led him to developing a psychotherapy that he named "Thought Field Therapy" (TFT). Other psychologists refined Callahan's methods. Emotional Freedom Techniques (EFT) was developed by Gary Craig and is the most well-known therapy that incorporated acupressure tapping into the treatments. There are too many acupressure based therapies and coaching methods to summarize here, but are described in the web site of the Association for Comprehensive Energy Psychology at Energypsych.org.

There are many criticisms of TFT, EFT, and energy psychology methods because there are not enough experimental studies that have met all the standards of science. The need for research studies is more important when the treatment interventions are novel and extremely different from conventional methods. Describing Psychological Reversals, energy meridians and incorporating acupressure is difficult to believe. There are many physicians, especially neurologists and psychologists, along with neuroscientists, professors and other clinicians and coaches who criticize the limited research in this area.

I have been involved with committees that review research for the last seven years. I first was trained in research in 1974 from Dr. Martin Seligman, who, when he became president of the American Psychological Association, was elected by the largest margin ever. From all my observations and involvements it is clear that, knowingly and unknowingly, academicians, scientists, mental health professionals and skeptics have not assisted or enabled such research to occur. Conducting such research of the highest experimental standards would not be extremely difficult. It simply would require the professionals listed above to give and facilitate access to doing such studies with a large number of participants. Ideally, this would be with college students. It should be noted, however, that there are an incredible amount of anecdotal reports and a growing number of research studies demonstrating that acupressure-based therapies and methods are extremely effective in reducing psychological problems and helping people reach their goals.

The stories in this book have illustrated some of the most important factors affecting performance levels at any moment and for periods of time. The importance of determination, getting the best coaching you can, making smart decisions, practicing and good general mental health cannot be overemphasized. Playing well under pressure, controlling negative emotions and correctly coming back from an injury are three major factors.

Performing Well Under Pressure: The importance of playing well under pressure is ubiquitous to all sports and often determines the difference between winning and losing, even though the athlete may be just one person on a team of more than 24. It is most pronounced at the end of a game, match, or competition. How athletes respond to pressure varies a great deal. This is true at any level of competition and is most pronounced with professional athletes. How many times have you heard that playing in one of golf's four majors is totally different than playing in any of the regular tour events? There is little or nothing to prepare almost all professional athletes for the adrenaline rush they will feel playing in a last and deciding game, such as the seventh game of an NBA championship or World Series. Winning one of the four major tennis titles can only occur not by playing it safe but by winning crucial points. It is very difficult, and essentially impossible, for practice sessions to create the amount and kind of pressure that occurs at the end of an important game or match. All coaches and managers practice different plays and strategies for different scenarios that could occur at the end of a match or game. Mistakes at that juncture can be made not only by players but by coaches, too, even veteran coaches. How many times have you seen an NFL coach botch the use of timeouts towards the end of the half or game?

Some of the most pronounced memories of avid sports fans about professional athletes will come from how those athletes perform at critical moments in competition. A great example of this is in Major League Baseball. The regular season starts in April and ends in October with the World Series determining the world champion. Greater world attention occurs during these games. A contrast between two great baseball hitters illustrates the importance of performing under pressure.

Alex Rodriguez had great regular-season hitting statistics. It earned him, in 2000, a salary of $252 million over 10 years, dwarfing all baseball contracts at the time. While Rodriguez is known for using steroids, the disparaging nickname of "Mr. May" was given to him before it was definitively known he had been playing on steroids. Why that nickname? Although a great hitter, Rodriguez consistently played poorly in October during the playoffs and World Series, with championships on the line. Similar to Rodriguez, Reggie Jackson also had excellent career statistics. But unlike Rodriguez he earned one of the greatest nicknames bestowed to any player in the history of the sport—"Mr. October"—primarily for his outstanding 1977 World Series for the New York Yankees. The highlight was Jackson hitting three home runs on three pitches off three pitchers in Game 6 of the series, helping the Yankees defeat the Los Angeles Dodgers.

Fans' memories of some athletes often involves how well they played under pressure. Robert Horry never played in an all-star game, but is easily remembered by basketball fans for hitting clutch shots at the end of a playoff game that were instrumental in being on teams that won 7 NBA championships on three different teams. Although his career statistics are slightly above average there has been recent conversation about his being voted into the Hall of Fame. No player with his career statistics in the modern era has been inducted into the Hall of Fame. Chris Weber was a five time NBA all-star, great score, and rebounder and smart enough to be one of the top analysts in basketball today. However, many fans will remember him as the player who panicked in the NCAA championship game when he called a time out when his team did not have any remaining. His team might have won the championship if he did not make this mistake. For those who are old enough, Bill Mazeroski will always be remembered for the walk off home run he hit in the seventh game to win the 1960 World Series. Kelly Strug will be remembered by gymnastic enthusiasts for her great vault despite having a severe ankle injury. That vault enabled the USA team to win the Olympic gold medal. In fact, the first footnote in Wikipedia about her is that "Kelly Strug's vault as part of the most memorable Olympic moments."

Performing well or poorly during critical moments is crucial and often determines who wins, no matter the level of competition. This is as true while playing in a foursome of golf at the country club as it is for a 16-year-old gymnast about to do her last event in what will determine whether her team advances to the Olympic Finals. How often have you been dying to beat someone for that very first time? You probably have been very close to winning, and it came down to how well you handled the pressure at the end of your match. If you're not good at such times, you usually keep on losing, losing and losing. If you're competitive, there is little solace in having a moral victory.

The lyrics to one of Billy Joel's most famous songs reflect this point.

But here you are in the ninth
Two men out and three men on
Nowhere to look but inside
Where we all respond to
Pressure, Pressure.

Having confidence in your ability at the end of a match is emphasized by all coaches. So is being advised to avoid having any negative thoughts. Any coach or teaching pro will encourage you to have positive thoughts and relax. However, there is nothing that any coach can say that can build up and sustain confidence like consistently performing well under the strain of pressure. PPO's ability to prevent the pressure of the moment to get to an athlete gives the player the best chance to excel. Being able to play and sustain greatness can then be experienced and enjoyed and remain a great lasting memory.

Not Letting Mistakes Cause Your Game to Decline: Everyone makes mistakes, hits a bad shot, or plays poorly at times. There is great variation in how players react to that, which can affect the rest of the match and determine who wins. It is almost impossible to play great throughout a match if mistakes cause your game to decline. It can cost you the match even if you are the superior athlete or player. This is especially true if the way you play continues to deteriorate for longer periods of time. Thus, the ability to recover quickly after hitting bad shots or making mistakes is an important part of mental toughness in any sport.

The deterioration of the level of play after making mistakes is one of the major reasons why amateur athletes and juniors do not get better results over time. When upset, it is difficult to focus on the next point. The body tightens up and self-criticism can run through your head. The improvement you developed through lessons and practice all of a sudden eludes you. Strategies previously thought out are forgotten or abandoned. In more extreme examples, players have been known to throw their golf clubs or even smash them into a tree. Tennis players, like myself, have at some point in time, smashed their rackets against the court or flung them in the air. Although it may temporarily discharge some of your anger, it is very difficult for a junior, country club or recreational player to get angrier and angrier and then maintain his or her level of play. There is no way to maintain consistency. Displays of temper usually empower the opponent and enable them to be more confident.

One strategy that your opponent may adopt is simply to keep the ball in play, nothing fancy, knowing that eventually you will make unforced errors.

Struggling with anger and temper is not limited to amateur athletes. There are many examples from professional sports. John Daly is a golfer with incredible talent. However, he would get so angry at himself after hitting bad shots that he periodically walked off the course in the middle of a PGA tournament. Even though he was playing in the prestigious 1999 Players Championship, he tossed his shoe into the crowd. Another time Daly became so angry that he took a spectator's camera and smashed it against a tree. When a good baseball pitcher knows that the batter is overly angry, tense and eager, it is usually good to pitch the ball initially near the strike zone and then out. Baseball Hall of Famer Greg Maddox used that strategy to help him win 355 games, eighth best all-time.

John McEnroe was the exception. He was perhaps the best tennis player in elevating his game when being angry. He swore at referees a number of times and called one a "jerk" during a match. McEnroe went on to defeat his arch-rival Bjorn Borg in a Wimbledon final even though he smashed his racket. "Superbrat," who was often booed, once yelled at a referee, "You cannot be *serious*." Ironically, this became one of the most famous phrases off the tennis courts and resulted in lucrative commercials for him.

Most professional athletes have the knack to not let bad shots or plays subsequently hurt their game. Some of the best cornerbacks in football are those who have short memories of the touchdown pass they just got beat on by the receiver. They focus in more deeply the next time they have to cover a receiver. A great basketball shooter, such as the Ray Allen, Stephen Curry and Michael Jordan can miss numerous shots at the beginning of the game, but keep on shooting until they finds their touch. After giving up a home run, great pitchers simply move on to getting out the next batter.

It is not simply having physical talent that enables athletes to quickly return to playing great. There are numerous psychological characteristics that make this possible. This is often currently referred to as "mental toughness." Examples of different aspects of mental toughness have been described a number of times in this book.

As pointed out in Chapter 1, coaches of the mental aspects of tennis emphasize for players to control their emotions, to let go of their anger, suspending judgment, forgetting past mistakes and getting into playing in the moment. Some coaches and authors de-emphasize the importance of winning and encourage players simply to focus on playing their best tennis. However, the vast majority of players very much care about winning, even though they did not play well in the game. Even the name of Brad Gilbert's popular book is "Winning Ugly". He was incredibly perceptive how to throw off an opponent's game and get them out of their flow. Many interesting and amusing stories are contained in this well written book. Whether it is a coach, manager, teaching pro of a country club or one who gives lessons periodically, teaching mental toughness is usually more important for some players than improving a forehand in tennis, hitting out of a bunker in golf, being able to hit to the opposite field in baseball or having a crossover dribble in basketball.

Coming Back After Injury: The most common mistake after getting injured is to try to come back too soon. This is especially true when it is your first serious injury. In team sports there is pressure from coaches and teammates to come back quickly. The biggest mistake made by adolescent and adult athletes is not following the guidelines given to you by your physical therapist, physician or trainer. Their recommendations are sometimes ignored or minimized. You may get overzealous when doing exercises that you have been given, maybe trying to lift heavier and heavier weights, only to re-aggravate the injury. Making matters worse, athletes sometimes then fail to report that setback to the trainers and coaches, trying instead to come back too quickly.

Get a guideline from the professional who is helping you to rehab your injury and follow it. You may have to rest the injury and then do light exercises. Pat Croce, one of the most famous physical therapists who eventually owned the Philadelphia 76ers, had a program of gradually warming up through light exercise followed by a combination of stretching, strengthening and stretching again, followed by icing the injury to reduce swelling. I am not putting it out there in any way that I am an expert in this area, but it is paramount to get the best advice for returning to sports for your particular injury.

Assuming all goes right, you will be guided to become more aggressive in the exercise program. A common phrase when exercising is "no pain, no gain." This usually does not apply in the early phases of the rehab process. If you avoid making these mistakes you are finally ready to get back to practicing and eventually playing in an actual game. Following this process enables you to recover as quickly as possible. You are not alone in having difficulties with the recovery process. Professional athletes make these mistakes. How many times have you seen a professional athlete re-aggravate an injury and then be disabled for a while or for the rest of the season?

Kevin Durant is a superb and multitalented basketball player. He was the National Basketball Association (NBA) leading scorer four times in five years. He has been first-team All-NBA for five straight years. This means he is considered one of the two best forwards in the entire league. He was the Most Valuable Player in 2014. He even was voted the best male athlete in the world in the annual ESPN awards. He sustained a broken bone at the base of his small toe during the preseason of 2014. The team's general manager, Sam Presti, former general manager of the year, commented that the team doctors identified the injury early on. He indicated that all were fortunate to catch the injury "on the front and, before this becomes more of an acute issue... We need to be in a position where we are thinking long term." Unfortunately Durant resumed basketball prematurely and then needed, not one, but two more surgeries. Durant did not play for the rest of the season and his team missed qualifying for the playoffs by one game. It is unclear if Durant will ever return to be the great player he had been throughout his career.

If it is clear to you and others that you don't seem to be recovering very well, it is a good idea to get a second opinion or consider some other option. Keep in mind that most medications will reduce pain and are necessary during certain phases of the recovery process, but you have to make sure you're recovering from the original injury.

Playing well under pressure, controlling negative emotions and properly and correctly coming back from an injury are not the only factors that optimize performance. Determination, practice, making smart decisions and good general mental health are some of the additional factors. The following are a few examples of how PPO has been instrumental in enhancing performance in other sports.

GOLF

Retired and More Time to Play Golf: Charlie T was a 58-year-old businessman who had a company that was bought out. He had enough money to never have to work again. He never imagined that to be possible, that he had pulled it off and that he had much more free time. Charlie became more involved in volunteering and being on the board of directors of two organizations. He and his wife were able to take more vacations, with some being longer than he had ever done in his life. His son and daughter did not live far away. Not only could he spend more time with them, but he was able to attend some of his grandchildren's sporting events and school plays. He was not much of a reader before selling his company but started getting interested in stories about past successful people.

Before selling his business, golf was generally played on the weekends, on vacation periodically with his wife and occasionally with his son and daughter. He regularly played with the same foursome at the country club and occasionally in the club's tournaments. Good friendships developed with those he had played with over the years, along with other members of the club. It was great to be playing and shooting the breeze with his friends and getting away from all the planning and worrying they might do about their business. He generally shot in the low 80s. He would have liked to have scored in the high 70s. Charlie was not that competitive with others went it came to golf. Although he had high standards for himself, this was not the case with golf. Now that he sold his business, Charlie had a lot more time for golf. Golf went from being a hobby to being a passion. He took more lessons and played or practiced at least five days a week. By doing this, he fully expected to improve his game. This basically meant to him that he could shoot consistently in the high 70s or even better. Unfortunately, this was not the case, and it frustrated him. In fact, there were days when he shot in the low 90s as he started to pressure himself to shoot better and his frustration interfered with his ability to play relaxed.

Because he did not have any extremely upsetting past experiences, the Future Perspective Protocol was used. Charlie pictured and thought about his continued poor play of shooting in the 90s. He felt frustrated and tense and gave a Distress Rating of 9. The four steps of the PPO procedure were applied with Steps 2 and 4 being CATS. His frustration went down, but he started to feel disappointed. Thus, this negative feeling had to be treated and fortunately was done so successfully. Charlie then played and resumed improving. He had two more sessions with me. Resolving his problem took only a few steps, so he quickly learned how to apply PPO to himself and never needed to come back, nor did I receive phone calls for additional sessions.

Rarely Winning in his Foursome: John C was a 44-year-old orthopedic surgeon who regularly had a Saturday morning foursome. He loved playing golf, being outside and being a source of good jokes. However, he had a competitive streak that he pretty much kept to himself. Although he generally shot in the mid-80s, John almost always came in second, third or fourth. There was always something that prevented him from winning. However, his most frequent pattern of not winning came when had or came near to the lead. That's when his game went south. This was especially true with his putting. When close to winning, he had too many distracting thoughts, would not read the breaks in the green as well and was excessively tight when striking the ball.

As this was a pretty consistent pattern, the best approach was to apply the Past Perspective Protocol. His most upsetting experience was of having blown a shot lead with only two more holes to go. He double bogeyed the 17th by driving into the deep rough and then three-putting. On the 18th he needed four putts, including missing one from 3 feet. He recalled feeling uptight on those last two holes and being embarrassed and annoyed with himself that he botched the rough right at the end. He had become progressively more aggravated as he continued to hit bad shot after bad shot.

What is important within the PPO session is how he felt at the moment he was re-living that experience in our session. John was angry enough at himself when recalling that experience that he gave a Distress Rating of 7. He did three tapping rounds using CATS for steps two and four. However, his distress only went down to a 5. I did not suspect that hypersensitivities or that energetic disorganization were present. Since anger was the predominant feeling, the next step was to apply a more specific tapping sequence. Since John was angry with himself, the tapping sequence of 4-5-10-5 was applied for steps two and four. Three rounds of PPO using the algorithm associated with anger eliminated all distress.

Because he no longer felt anger when thinking about this past experience, he went on to the Future Perspective Protocol. We decided to change what could occur in the future to create a slightly different scenario. John projected about having a five-stroke lead on all three players with three holes to go. He felt nervous at that moment in the session and gave a distress rating of 5. As such, he tapped on the acupressure points that are associated with anxiety. He tapped on acupressure points 6-7-5-10-5. Although the two tapping rounds dissipated his anger, a third round should be done and was utilized.

To try to eliminate the problem further, I asked John to think about playing with the senior partner in his orthopedic practice. He was a much better golfer and John did not anticipate that he would beat him. However, his partner was somewhat of a braggart and John knew he would poke fun at him in front of colleagues and friends on how he thoroughly beat John. This elicited more anger. The tapping sequence 4-5-10-5 quickly eliminated this distressing feeling. Five weeks later, John called to tell me that he had not only finally won in his foursome, but had done so one additional time. When he played with his senior partner, John did not win, but did more than hold his own. Although still subjected to his partner's condescending and annoying comments, it did not bother him.

This is an example when using CATS is not sufficient and required the application of more specific tapping sequences.

BASEBALL

A Pitcher Becomes Ineffective: Anthony was an 18-year-old college pitcher who had very good control and quickly became the team's third starter even though he was a freshman. However, he suddenly and inexplicably lost his ability to locate his pitches over a series of starts. Video of his pitching enabled him and his coach to analyze and try to correct his mechanics. Coaches provided good advice. He knew he needed to stay calm and focus on his next pitch when he was having difficulty or had just made a costly mistake. He was told to stay calm and to trust his natural ability. Anthony's inability to do this made everything worse. Not only was he removed from the starting rotation, but essentially was not pitching at all. Anthony's parents had him start meeting me and we worked over the Internet.

Given how upset he was and his loss of confidence, we first started working with the Past Perspective Protocol. He picked a number of times when he had pitched horribly. In almost every memory, his first response was to be very angry with himself. PPO could not eliminate all the negative feelings. He had about those experiences. Similar to Novak Djokovic, it turned out that he was extremely sensitive to gluten. When I tested for this possibility, applied, kinesiology determined that his muscles weakened when simply thinking and verbalizing about gluten products, such as bread, spaghetti, and pizza. Anthony was very committed to improving and read about and changed his diet. The next PPO session went smoothly because he stopped eating gluten products. He felt calm when thinking about any of the past upsetting experiences.

In preparation for pitching in the future, Anthony wanted to picture himself as a starter. However, it is important to think out what the sequence of events will be in the future. It was not like he would simply be reinstated as a starting pitcher. His coaches could see that he was displaying better control pitching and getting better results. The PPO sessions helped. As expected, his coaches first started him back as a relief pitcher. Anthony was no longer getting rattled and filled with self-doubt when he made some bad pitches or getting angry and flustered when his teammates made errors that cost runs. Anthony started to make regular appearances as a relief pitcher throughout the rest of that year. Although he did not become a starter or the closer, his coaches had him pitch in more games and his earned run average was a very low 1.29 over his last four appearances. I never found out how he did in subsequent years.

Getting Out of a Hitting Slump: Kevin K. was a 17-year-old junior who was one of the best hitters on his high school baseball team and was the starting second baseman. He and his parents contacted me after he had been in an extended hitting slump, going 1-for-15 in his last four games – and the only hit was a single. This also affected his fielding as he made two uncharacteristic errors in the field. He repeatedly watched videos of his hitting during games. He started to doubt his abilities and felt uncomfortable at the plate. And, as many batters do who are in a slump, he was overthinking how to correct his problems.

Kevin was too uptight, embarrassed and frustrated and I decided to not have him do PPO with the Future Perspective Protocol. He went back to his most recent game with the Past Perspective Protocol, when he had gone 0-4, left three players stranded in scoring position and made a costly error that contributed to his team's loss. He had been put down in the order from second to seventh hitter. When he thought about all of this in our session, Kevin felt upset enough with himself that he gave this a rating of 8. After tapping to remove the psychological reversals, three entire rounds of the four-step PPO procedure, his Distress Rating went down to a 2. After the Eye Roll procedure, he fell completely relaxed. Others told him to not put too much pressure on himself and Kevin knew that. However, knowing it does not necessarily translate into being able to do it. He reported feeling different about it and only felt confident after the session.

I then had him take the Future Perspective Protocol of his hitting in the upcoming playoff games. I asked him to imagine that he was hitting with runners on second and third and two outs in the bottom of the seventh inning against his team's rival high school team. He immediately felt anxious, at the level of a 6. The treatment quickly eliminated his nervousness. He did have to use the Eye Roll Procedure to get his Distress Rating to zero. Kevin used PPO before or during a game and hit .444 for the rest of the season. He was a conscientious and determined young man. Although he did not make any of the All-County teams, he was very pleased that he hit better for the remainder of the season.

BASKETBALL

Improving Foul Shooting: Jayla B. was a 19-year-old senior who started and was a captain on her high school basketball team. She was averaging 14.9 points and 4.4 assists. She was also hoping to get at least a partial scholarship to play basketball in college. Although she shot 48% from the field, her foul shooting average was only 44%, where a very good point guard in high school should be shooting at least 67% from the foul line. Her free-throw shooting was especially bad at the end of the game. This poor foul shooting was in contrast to how well she did in practice.

Jasmine was another example of having to apply a specific tapping sequence. Jasmine used the Past Perspective Protocol in a game from two weeks earlier. She had been fouled with 11 seconds to go with the score tied. She missed both foul shots by coming up short and hitting the front of the rim, usually a sign of being too tense. Unfortunately, the other team came down and scored to win the game. It was not easy to get her to recognize her feelings in our session. If she was working on PPO by herself, she simply would have done CATS for Steps 2 and 4. We tried that in our session, but it was not helpful. After talking with her, I helped Jasmine to realize that she was actually feeling embarrassed about blowing the game. After tapping to remove the psychological reversals, she tapped on the relevant acupressure points of 2-5-10-5. This decreased her embarrassment. Interestingly enough, she then started feeling angry with herself. As such, we switched the acupressure tapping sequence to 4-5-10-5. After dissipating her anger, I had her continue to think about that game. By simply reducing the anger she felt, her embarrassment went down to a 1. It is not unusual for the Distress Rating of the first negative emotion, in this case embarrassment, to go down even though the tapping focused on tapping for the second emotion, anger. We only needed one more round of tapping on the acupressure points associated with embarrassment to remove any negative feelings or body sensations even when she was thinking about missing the foul shots that led to her team losing.

She then used the Future Perspective Protocol about shooting fouls at the end of the game. She was feeling tense and rated this as an 8. This feeling was easily removed when the sequence of acupressure points tapped was 6-7-5-10-5. To help generalize the results, I had her think of playing in front of a packed gym at her high school, with her team down one point with 2 seconds remaining in a game that would determine if her team would make the playoffs. Jasmine felt somewhat nervous and rated this as a 4. This nervousness was no longer present after using the tapping sequence of 6-7-5-10-5. She mad 64.3% of her foul shots for the remainder of the season.

Coming Back from Injury: Calvin was a 16-year-old basketball player who was the starting point guard for his high school team. Unfortunately, he tore his anterior cruciate ligament (ACL). Surgery was successful, but it was very difficult for him to be so inactive after the surgery. When finally going into physical therapy, he was surprised and annoyed at how light the weights were used to rehab his knee. Calvin tried to recover too quickly by adding weights in the exercises when training at the gym. He also returned to playing competitive basketball before his knee healed sufficiently. He did not think it was a problem because he was back to running and jumping, and figured he would continue to improve. Unfortunately, his knee injury got worse. Calvin felt a popping sensation and was terrified that he re-tore his ACL. Fortunately, it was an aggravation of the injury. But now he was back in physical therapy. Although not exactly back to ground zero, he was back to light weights. And now it would take longer before he could play again.

He followed doctors' orders and became more conscientious and patient in his rehabilitation. Calvin gradually recovered, but the aggravation of the injury caused him to miss almost all of the following season. Calvin went to basketball camps that summer. He knew that college coaches and assistants were scouting high school players. Calvin knew that this was an opportunity to impress them and possibly get scholarship offers. In the first summer camp, Calvin was fearful of tearing his ACL again and it caused him to be more hesitant. Calvin had been a point guard who was very quick and good at handling the ball. He did not have a great jump shot and was best at penetrating and dishing off to other players for open shots. Because he was unsure if he would get injured again, he did not drive to the basket and took too many jump shots that he missed. None of the coaches contacted him after that camp.

It was at this point that I was contacted. Calvin complained about being fearful he would injure his knee again and was no longer confident in his game. In our session, it was apparent that the Past Perspective Protocol was needed in having him re-live the moment that he injured his knee and the time he had the popping sensation. He became fearful in the session and had a Distress Rating of 9. We did two rounds of PPO using CATS for steps two and four. When his distress only went down to a 2 after the second round, the Eye Roll Procedure was done and completely eliminated any negative feelings or body sensations he had. As always, he did a third tapping round

Calvin then took the future perspective where he projected himself playing in front of college coaches at the summer camp that was coming up in three weeks. As an additional stressor for him, but also for providing better preparation, I had him picture not playing well and that coaches were talking to other players, but not him. After three rounds of PPO, he no longer felt apprehension or any tension in his body.

He then played quite well at the summer camp. He was moving well and was penetrating successfully, putting up floaters or distributing the ball to cutting teammates for assists. A number of assistant coaches and two head coaches contacted him and his family and watched him play his senior year. Calvin was offered three partial scholarships and ended up going to and playing for a Division II college team.

GYMNASTICS

The Young Gymnastic Enthusiast: Ashley was a 8-year-old girl who had been going to a gymnastics academy for the past two years. She was not interested in other sports. The entire family was passionate about gymnastics. Like her older sister, Ashley lived and breathed gymnastics. She was funny, outgoing and well-liked by her friends. She fantasized about winning the gold medal in the Olympics, with "my parents and the whole world watching me receive the gold medal."

Ashley was considered the most skilled gymnast, not only for her age, but even for girls one year older than her. She loved and was excited that her gymnastics skills were almost as good as her older sister's. Unfortunately, she had done poorly at her County competitions, not performing close to her level that she exhibited in practice. This did not sit well with her parents, who were perfectionists in their own careers as lawyers. Ashley and the instructors well understood that her parents were disappointed in her. They would all emphasize to Ashley to be more focused, and would try to build her confidence. Although her parents would emphasize to Ashley that she simply needed to relax, it was clearly communicated in a pressured way. Ashley complained of feeling very tense at the competitions and reported that she could not stop thoughts racing through her mind before and during the routines.

I only needed to work with Ashley for one session. It is not unusual to get very quick results with young children. They don't try to figure out what this acupressure method is about. I simply presented it as a form of the game "Simon says," without having to say "Simon says" before telling her what to do. We used the past perspective. And when Ashley thought about how poorly she had done in the past competition, she was clearly frustrated with herself. Frustration is often experienced as anger. As such, she tapped the acupressure points of 4-5-10-5 and only needed one round of the PPO method to eliminate her anger. She then was asked to think about future competition and Ashley reported feeling nervous. As such, the acupressure points 6-5-10-5 were tapped and she felt relaxed after the one round of PPO. Ashley did quite well in the subsequent competitions. She easily remembered what acupressure points to tap and applied PPO to herself before the competitions.

The Joy of the Sport: Let's not forget the simple joy of playing any sport. When we all started playing the game and continued to pursue it, it was because we enjoyed it. Sometimes competitiveness, parental pressure or unrelenting standards you have for yourself cause you to get away from enjoying the game. The pleasure and fun that you used to have for the game can become a far distant second to your desire to excel. PPO can enable you to recapture the joy and love of the game.

Here is a way to help yourself. When doing PPO, always think about what it is that you want, but do not have. If you realize that you have not been enjoying playing tennis or any sport for quite a while, that becomes the structure for setting up and applying the PPO session. For instance, you might think of a time when you really loved playing the game. Stay with that memory for a while. Recall what it was that you enjoyed the most! Now take some time to think about what it has been like lately. You then may feel dissatisfied, disappointed or other emotions. Notice the negative feeling or body sensation you have at this moment and give it a Distress Rating. You then apply the PPO method.

You usually will have to apply the past perspective first and then the future perspective protocol. You will usually find that it helps reduce the negative feeling in the session. More importantly you likely will find yourself enjoying the game when you subsequently play. Sometimes that good feeling has not decreased as much as you would like. Just go back a later day and repeat the PPO method and notice the positive feelings emerge.

One More Thing to Keep in Mind: Peak Performance Optimization is a method that enhances performance. It is not limited to sports. People have been helped with performing better in scholastic tests, business, executive decision-making, public speaking, writing and the performing arts. Go to **PerformAtPeak.com** for more information about what other areas of functioning that PPO helps.

This is an incredible method that helps reduce so many problems and simultaneously increases your level of performance. You have an opportunity to develop a skill that can dramatically help you. I will emphasize again that it may be initially somewhat difficult to get used to it, but will clearly be of great benefit

Stop and think about the following:

Think about past times when you were developing an ability, learning a skill that was initially difficult and required a good amount of time to develop. When you think about being in school, remember how long and hard you would study for tests that ultimately only made a little amount of difference in your overall school record and what college or graduate program you ended up attending.

Reflect on past experiences you have had in business. How hard and how much effort was needed to complete a past project? How much persistence did you need?

How many times did you write and rewrite a speech and then repeatedly practiced giving it? What were the benefits that you reaped?

For those in the performing arts, how hard was it to get to how good you are now? How difficult was it initially and throughout these past years?

Use that same persistence to become skilled at applying PPO. Once you learn how to apply PPO, you will likely get the greatest and expedient improvement compared to other methods. You can apply it quickly, at almost any time and in whatever situation where performance is important.

I am always interested in reading about your experiences. Please feel free to write about them and email to **Stories@PerformAtPeak.com**.

APPENDIX 1

APPLYING PPO USING THE FUTURE PERSPECTIVE PROTOCOL

Applying PPO Using the Future Perspective Protocol

It is highly recommended that you photocopy this appendix before beginning. You will then have extra copies to use any time you want to apply PPO again

Think about and picture your biggest problem in tennis. Think about playing an opponent you are competitive with. Imagine playing quite well and then all of a sudden your problem is occurring and you can't get it to stop. Then you start to make a number of different mistakes and are playing poorly. Keep in mind that this problem has been occurring and will occur in the future.

Greater activation of negative feelings will help PPO to more fully decrease your problem. You can picture this experience as a photograph, or see it occurring over time as you would with a video.

Describe this problem that you want to overcome.

_____

_____

_____

_____

_____

_____

Write the emotion or body sensations you are having right now at this moment. You are not too write down what you were feeling during that experience. What counts is the current feelings you are now experiencing.

_____

_____

_____

_____

How intense are you experiencing the negative emotion at this moment? Give a rating from 0-10.

Distress Rating = _____

1) Eliminate the three Psychological Reversals:

Tap on the karate spot (Acupressure Point 1) and say three times:

"I deeply and profoundly accept myself with all my problems and limitations."

Pause a few seconds. Tap on the karate spot on the other hand (Acupressure Point 1) and say three times:

"Even though I have this problem, I deeply accept myself."

Tap under your nose (Acupressure Point 2) and say three times:

"I deeply accept myself even if I never get completely over this problem."

Distress Rating = _____

(Recall that your Distress Rating may not go down from treating the reversals. This procedure removes the blocks that impede progress.)

2) Apply CATS by tapping on Acupressure Points:

3-4-5-6-7-5-8-9-2-11-5-10-5.

How intense are you experiencing the negative emotion at this moment? Give a rating from 0-10.

Distress Rating = _____

3) Brain Balance Procedure:

While you continuously tap on the 10th Acupressure Point, you are to simultaneously:

a) Close your eyes.
b) Open your eyes and look straight ahead.
c) Move your eyes to 5:00 on a clock by looking down to your right.
d) Move your eyes to 7:00 on a clock, by looking down to your left.
e) Circle your eyes clockwise for two revolutions.
f) Circle your eyes counterclockwise for two revolutions.
g) Hum high and low notes without words.
h) Count to 5 out loud.
i) Hum high and low notes.

How intense are you experiencing the negative emotion or body sensation at this moment? Give a rating from 0-10.

Distress Rating = _____

4) Apply CATS by tapping on Acupressure Points:

3-4-5-6-7-5-8-9-2-11-5-10-5.

How intense are you experiencing the negative emotion or body sensations at this moment? Give rating from 0-10.

Distress Rating = _____

If your Distress Rating is a 1 or 2, do the Eye Roll Procedure.

You have now completed one round of PPO for this negative emotion or body sensation. Even if your Distress Rating is zero, you still are to do three rounds.

You will now follow the same steps as you did in the first round.

Second Round

1) Eliminate the Specific Psychological Reversal:

Tap on the karate spot (Acupressure Point 1) and say three times:

"Even though I have this problem, I deeply accept myself."

Distress Rating = _____

2) Apply the CATS Procedure.

Distress Rating = _____

3) Do Brain Balance Procedure.

    Distress Rating = _____

4) Apply the CATS Procedure

    Distress Rating = _____

If the Distress Rating is a 1 or 2, apply the Eye Roll Procedure.

    Distress Rating = _____

Even if your Distress Rating is zero, you still are to do the third round.

Third Round

1) Eliminate the Specific Psychological Reversal:

Tap on the karate spot (Acupressure Point 1) and say three times:

"Even though I have this problem, I deeply accept myself."

    Distress Rating = _____

2 Apply the CATS Procedure

    Distress Rating = _____

3) Do Brain Balance Procedure.

    Distress Rating = _____

4) Apply the CATS Procedure.

    Distress Rating = _____

If your Distress Rating is a 1 or 2, do the Eye Roll Procedure.

Important Assessment: If your Distress Rating is zero or a 1, then you are ready to go out to the court and play. Enjoy!

Guidelines on what to do when your Distress Rating is 2 or above:

Is your Distress Rating 2 or above? If you are still feeling the same emotion, apply the Past Perspective Protocol described below.

If your Distress Rating is 2 or above, notice if the emotion you are currently experiencing is different than what you felt when you started this Future Perspective Protocol. If you are feeling a different emotion, apply this Future Perspective Protocol for this new emotion. You can write your answers on one of the copies of Appendix 1.

Once you have finished the three rounds of tapping for this new emotion what is your

Distress Rating = _____

If your Distress Rating is a zero or one, then you are ready to go out to the court and play. Enjoy!

If your Distress Rating is 2 or above, apply the Past Perspective Protocol as described below.

APPENDIX 2

APPLYING THE PPO USING THE PAST PERSPECTIVE PROTOCOL

It is highly recommended that you photocopy this appendix before beginning. You will then have extra copies to use any time you want to apply PPO again. You can write your answers below. You can go to appendix 2 and photocopy it.

Picture and think about the worst experience you had in the past when your problem occurred. Give yourself time to reflect on this memory. Try to remember it clearly as if it happened to you yesterday. Try to remember the most upsetting times in that entire experience. Keep doing so to activate a negative emotion or body sensation. Greater activation of negative feelings will help PPO to more fully decrease your problem. When thinking about this upsetting experience, you can picture it as a photograph or see it occurring over time as you would with a video.

Write down about that experience:

_____

_____

_____

_____

Write the emotion or body sensations you are having right now at this moment. You are not too write down what you were feeling during that experience. What counts is the current feelings you are now experiencing.

_____

_____

_____

_____

How intense are you experiencing the negative emotion at this moment? Give a rating from 0-10.

Distress Rating = _____

1) Eliminate the Psychological Reversals:

Tap on the karate spot (Acupressure Point 1) and say three times:

"I deeply and profoundly accept myself with all my problems and limitations."

Pause a few seconds. Tap on the karate spot on the other hand (Acupressure Point 1) and say three times:

"Even though I have this problem, I deeply accept myself."

Tap under your nose (Acupressure Point 2) and say three times:

"I deeply accept myself even if I never get completely over this problem."

Distress Rating = _____

(Recall that your Distress Rating may not go down from treating the reversals. This procedure removes the blocks that impede progress.)

2) Apply CATS by tapping on Acupressure Points:

3-4-5-6-7-5-8-9-2-11-5-10-5.

How intense are you experiencing the negative emotion at this moment? Give a rating from 0-10.

    Distress Rating = _____

3) Brain Balance Procedure:

While you continuously tap on the 10th Acupressure Point, you are to simultaneously:

   a) Close your eyes.
   b) Open your eyes and look straight ahead.
   c) Move your eyes to 5:00 on a clock by looking down to your right.
   d) Move your eyes to 7:00 on a clock, by looking down to your left.
   e) Circle your eyes clockwise for two revolutions.
   f) Circle your eyes counterclockwise for two revolutions.
   g) Hum high and low notes without words.
   h) Count to 5 out loud.
   i) Hum high and low notes.

How intense are you experiencing the negative emotion or body sensation at this moment? Give a rating from 0-10.

    Distress Rating = _____

4) Apply CATS by tapping on Acupressure Points:

3-4-5-6-7-5-8-9-2-11-5-10-5.

How intense are you experiencing the negative emotion or body sensations at this moment? Give rating from 0-10.

Distress Rating = _____

If your Distress Rating is 2 or less, do the Eye Roll Procedure.

You have now completed one round of PPO for this negative emotion or body sensation. Even if your Distress Rating is zero, you still are to do three rounds.

You will now follow the same steps as you did in the first round.

Second Round

1) Eliminate the Specific Psychological Reversal:

Tap on the karate spot (Acupressure Point 1) and say three times:

"Even though I have this problem, I deeply accept myself."

Distress Rating = _____

2) Apply the CATS Procedure.

Distress Rating = _____

3) Do Brain Balance Procedure.

Distress Rating = _____

4) Apply the CATS Procedure

Distress Rating = _____

If the Distress Rating is a 1 or 2, apply the Eye Roll Procedure.

Distress Rating = _____

Even if your Distress Rating is zero, you still are to do the third round.

Third Round

1) Eliminate the Specific Psychological Reversal:

Tap on the karate spot (Acupressure Point 1) and say three times:

"Even though I have this problem, I deeply accept myself."

> Distress Rating = _____

2 Apply the CATS Procedure

> Distress Rating = _____

3) Do Brain Balance Procedure.

> Distress Rating = _____

4) Apply the CATS Procedure.

> Distress Rating = _____

If your Distress Rating is a 1 or 2, do the Eye Roll Procedure.

Important Assessment: If your Distress Rating using the past perspective is zero or 1, you will apply the Future Perspective Protocol. You can write your answers on one of your photocopies of the Future Perspective Protocol.

If your Distress Rating is not zero or 1 you will repeat the Past Procedure Protocol in reference to the second worst experience you had with the this problem. You can write your answers on one your photocopies of the Past Perspective Protocol.

If you have applied the Past Perspective Protocol two times:

No matter what your Distress Rating is after applying the Past Perspective Protocol an additional time, you then apply the Future

Perspective Protocol. After completing this when thinking of your problem in the future, you are to go out and play tennis even if your Distress Rating is 2 or above.

You can reap the benefits of PPO the more that you apply and get accustomed to this method.

APPENDIX 3

Chart of Tapping Points

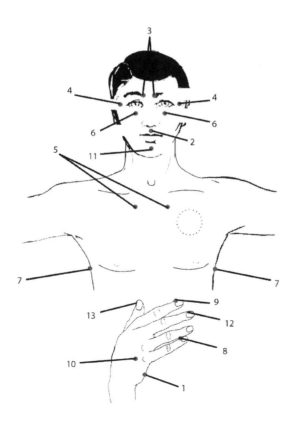

APPENDIX 4

LINKS TO WATCH VIDEOS OF THE PPO PROCEDURES

- Book.PerformAtPeak.com and click on "Psychological Reversals"
  This video also demonstrates the elimination of Psychological Reversals and how the testing of muscle strength (Applied Kinesiology) provided information about the energy in the body.
- Book.PerformAtPeak.com and click on "Comprehensive Acupressure Tapping Sequence (CATS)"
- Book.PerformAtPeak.com and click on "Brain Balance Procedure"
- Book.PerformAtPeak.com and click on "One Round of PPO"
- Book.PerformAtPeak.com and click on "Simplified Collarbone Breathing Technique"
- Book.PerformAtPeak.com and click on "Energy Neutralization Technique"

Use the QR code to your right to watch the video of the PPO procedures.

INDEX

Made in the USA
Middletown, DE
26 June 2015